ALL YOU NEED
TO BELIEVE

Foundations

OF THE *Faith*

The Apostles' Creed

ALL YOU NEED

TO BELIEVE

C. Donald Cole

MOODY PRESS
CHICAGO

To my wife, Naomi,
who helped me understand
the Apostles' Creed

CONTENTS

INTRODUCTION

*C*hristians who recite the Apostles' Creed every Sunday take it for granted that the Creed belongs in the worship service. Other Christians, brought up in churches where the Creed is not recited, question its usefulness. They prefer passages straight from the Bible. Which of the two opinions is better?

I shall not attempt to answer. In churches where the Creed is loved, Christians will go on reciting it. But the Creed is such a profound compendium of Christian truth that *thoughtful* recitation would take considerably longer than can be spared in a Sunday morning service. My purpose in this book is to examine thoughtfully the great biblical truths enshrined in the Creed and to apply them to our lives.

> I believe in God the Father Almighty,
> Maker of heaven and earth:
> And in Jesus Christ, His only Son, our Lord,

Who was conceived by the Holy Ghost,
Born of the Virgin Mary,
Suffered under Pontius Pilate,
Was crucified, dead, and buried:
He descended into hell;
The third day He rose from the dead;
He ascended into heaven,
And sitteth on the right hand of God the Father
    Almighty;
From thence He shall come to judge the quick and
    the dead.
I believe in the Holy Ghost:
The holy catholic church,
The communion of saints:
The forgiveness of sins:
The resurrection of the body,
And the life everlasting.

Amen.

Why did the early Fathers think it necessary to formulate a theological statement of biblical—especially New Testament—teaching?

At least four reasons can be given:

1. To present the truth of the gospel in concise form.
2. To refute heresy.
3. To act as the basis of ecclesiastical fellowship.
4. To ensure consistent teaching on the part of those who otherwise might contradict each other.

These reasons are just as valid today as in the first centuries of Christian history. Even churches that do not customarily use the Apostles' Creed prepare statements of faith. Sometimes they are quite lengthy, covering such topics as baptism, church order, and the Lord's second coming. These are not really creeds, but confessions. Whereas the great creeds proclaim truth that unites believers of all denominations, church confessions emphasize denominational distinctives.

In the early church the Creed was necessary in order to correct, among other things, faulty views of Christ's nature. At first, Peter's great confession was sufficient. "Thou art the Christ, the Son of the living God," he said (Matthew 16:16, KJV). But error crept into the church, and Peter's confession had to be amplified. What kind of man was this Christ, the Son of God?

Not until the middle of the fifth century was the theological statement about the nature of Christ complete. By then, various councils had dealt with heretical views that surfaced from time to time. Two of the most important were the Nicene Council of A.D. 325 and the Council of Chalcedony in A.D. 451. The Nicene Creed defended the doctrine of the deity of Christ against Arius, an early heretic. The Chalcedony Creed affirms what Christians have always believed, that Christ had two natures in one person.

Whether your church (or mine) recites the creeds, we are all indebted to the godly men who formulated them. As A. A. Hodge says, the creeds are "the common heritage of the whole Church."[1] They give content to our confessions of faith. Consequently, when we say, "Thou art the Christ, the Son of the living God," or "Jesus is Lord," we know what we are saying. And if we are true believers, we also mean it when we say:

I believe in ... Jesus Christ,
[God's] only Son, our Lord ...

NOTE

1. A. A. Hodge, *The Confession of Faith* (Edinburgh: Banner of Truth, 1869),
   5.

Chapter One

BELIEF IN
GOD IS PERSONAL

I believe in God the Father Almighty,
Maker of heaven and earth …

The Apostles' Creed begins simply yet profoundly: "I believe …" With that beginning, the Creed supports the biblical truth that faith in God is personal. It is each person's statement of faith, calling the reciter to witness to what he personally believes.

A person does not subscribe to the Creed because he is a member of a church that holds to it: instead, he already believes the truth stated in the Creed before associating himself with a church that professes it. "I believe," he says, and on the basis of his personal testimony, he is received into the fellowship.

A Christian church is a community of believers; every member believes the same basic truths as revealed in the Bible. Otherwise they would not gather together, for "what has a believer in common with an unbeliever?"

(2 Corinthians 6:15). Hence, the Creed is an expression of their belief by virtue of its having been first an expression of the personal faith of each member.

The importance of this truth cannot be overstated. Belief in God through our Lord Jesus Christ is utterly personal. Unless one understands this, sooner or later the practice of religion becomes tedious. This happens in many lives. Teenagers drop out of Sunday school because it bores them. Adults fall away because the sermons meet no conscious need.

In some cases the sermons are pointed. The listeners understand but reject the truth. They are like the wicked of Psalm 10, who "do not care about the Lord; in their pride they think that God doesn't matter" (Psalm 10:4, TEV).

There is little hope for men and women who think that God does not matter. There *is* hope for men and women who think that God *does* matter, but who do not yet know Him personally. Having been reared in a church, they assume that their church membership safeguards their future. The truth is, they are as lost *in* the church as the unchurched are *outside* it.

Salvation belongs only to those who internalize the truth of the gospel, those who turn from their sin and in faith ask Christ to come into their lives. They are genuine Christians, responding to Christ's call. They heed the apostle who says, "If *you* confess with your mouth Jesus as Lord, and believe in *your* heart that God raised Him from the dead, *you* shall be saved" (Romans 10:9, emphasis added).

If *you* do this, you will be able to recite the Creed truthfully:

I believe in God ...

14

Chapter Two

"I BELIEVE

IN GOD"

I believe in *God* the Father Almighty,
Maker of heaven and earth ...

*I*t is not always easy to believe in God. Sometimes we feel like the man who cried out, "I do believe; but help me not to doubt!" (Mark 9:24 NLT). Only those who sense a deep need for God really believe. Others accept the idea of God without actually committing themselves to Him, or they dismiss Him as a superstition no longer tolerable in the age of science. It is necessary to thirst for God in order to believe in Him (Psalm 42:2), and in the Apostles' Creed we express our belief.

None of us reasoned the way to God. The Bible makes no effort whatsoever to prove that God is; it assumes His existence.

However, there is ample evidence to support the probability of God. Christians find it convincing. The evidence is also damning, because those who ignore it have no excuse for their refusal to believe in God.

Consider the rationality of the universe. Its existence gives evidence for a thinking, reasoning Creator. Theologians usually discuss the rationality of the universe under four headings.

The first is *cosmology*. The dictionary defines *cosmology* as "that branch of metaphysics which treats the character of the universe as an orderly system, or cosmos." Only an almighty God could have produced the universe as we know it.

The second heading is *teleology*. Teleology is "the doctrine or belief that design is apparent in nature." Nature's design is too complex for things to have just happened or evolved. Behind the functioning of nature is an intelligent Creator.

The third is *anthropology*. This is the science or study of man. Christians believe that man is the chief evidence of design in the universe. Of all the creatures, he alone is able to understand that design. Thus, man, like his Creator, is intelligent.

Man also has personality. Can anyone really believe that man is an accident, a chance collision of matter? Since we cannot produce something from nothing, a person cannot have evolved from an impersonal source. Thus, the God who made man must be personal.

The fourth heading is *ontology*. The dictionary defines *ontology* as "the science of being or reality; the branch of knowledge that investigates the nature, essential properties, and relations of beings." According to this argument, man's striving for perfection is evidence of a perfect source—God Himself. We are imperfect creatures living in an imperfect world. Where did we get our concept of perfection, if not from the source of life, God Himself?

There is only one explanation for the nature of man: creation by a perfect God. As David wrote many centuries ago: "O Lord, You have searched me and known me. . . . For You formed my inward parts; You wove me in my mother's womb. I will give thanks to You, for I am fearfully and wonderfully made" (Psalm 139:1, 13–14).

Better, perhaps, than any intellectual argument for the existence of God is the Christian's experience of Him. As David also said, "How precious also are Your thoughts to me, O God! How vast is the sum of them! If I should count them, they would outnumber the sand. When I awake, I am still with You" (Psalm 139:17–18). Hence, we can say individually and unitedly,

I believe in *God* . . .

Chapter Three

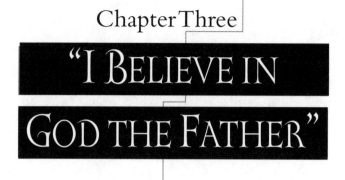

"I BELIEVE IN GOD THE FATHER"

I believe in God the *Father* Almighty ...

The Creed does not permit belief in God as an abstract force. It states simply but firmly, "I believe in God the Father." What does this term imply? The answer is partially given through the story of the Prodigal Son (Luke 15:11–32).

The Prodigal Son is perhaps the best-known story of the Bible. What family does not have its own "prodigal son," and perhaps a prodigal daughter as well? The younger son in the story was worse than a spendthrift; he was thoroughly rebellious and wayward. His squandering of his father's money was symptomatic of a disease of the soul. But eventually he came to his senses and returned to his old father, whom he had forsaken so callously.

That beloved story, however, is more than the spiritual odyssey of a young man. The central revelation concerns the character of the father. The miracle is that the father never stopped waiting for his son and was willing to take him in when he came home. Every family has its prodigal son, but not many fathers are as loving and forgiving as that father. The son is what literary critics might call an archetype (that is, a type which occurs frequently in life and literature). The father is not an archetype; he is a rarity.

God is like that father who ran to meet his returning son. Or, better yet, the father is like God, who welcomes sinners home to His heart. This is no doubt one of the loveliest truths of the Bible. God is our Father.

God is Father in two distinct senses: He is the Father of all humankind by creation, and He is the Father of Christians by redemption. This is a most important distinction. Non-Christians are not entitled to address God in prayer as "Our Father who art in heaven." In their case, He is Father only in the sense that He is the source of all life—their Creator.

Paul quotes approvingly a Greek poet who said, "For we also are His children" (Acts 17:28). And in Ephesians Paul says he bowed his knees "before the Father, from whom every family in heaven and on earth derives its name" (Ephesians 3:14–15).

Yet He is Father in the redemptive sense, and the Bible notes this truth about the character of God. The story of the Prodigal Son dramatizes this aspect of His character: there He is, waiting with outstretched arms for His wayward children to repent and come home. All who turn from their evil ways and return to Him in faith find the warm embrace of a Father in heaven.

The concept of God as Father does not begin in the New Testament, but in the Old. When our Lord taught

His disciples to pray, "Our Father who art in heaven," He was not talking about something entirely new to them. Their Hebrew Old Testament revealed that God wished to establish a father-son relationship with His ancient people. He tried, even though He seems not to have succeeded.

That is evident in David's conversation with his son Solomon. David told Solomon that God had denied him the privilege of building the temple; Solomon would build it instead. God said to David, "A son shall be born to you, who shall be a man of rest. . . . He shall build a house for My name, and he shall be My son and I will be his father" (1 Chronicles 22:9–10).

Earlier God had taught David to call Him his Father. In a passage that really looks beyond David to the Messiah, God says, "He will cry to Me, 'You are my Father, my God, and the rock of my salvation'" (Psalm 89:26). But there isn't much evidence in the Old Testament that David or anyone else was truly conscious of the fatherhood of God. They called upon Him as Adonai and Jehovah, but seldom as their Father.

God yearned for such a friendship. Israel spurned it. Through the prophet Isaiah, God complained about Israel's coldness of heart. "Sons I have reared and brought up, but they have revolted against Me," says the Lord (Isaiah 1:2). A moment later, God laments: "Alas, sinful nation, people weighed down with iniquity, offspring of evildoers, sons who act corruptly! They have abandoned the Lord, they have despised the Holy One of Israel, they have turned away from Him" (Isaiah 1:4).

God called His people "sons who act corruptly." That may be the source of our Lord's parable of the

Prodigal Son. The people of ancient Israel, whom God wished to bring up as sons, rejected His fatherhood. There were a few exceptions. Isaiah, for example, called upon God as Father. He prayed, "For You are our Father . . . You, O Lord, are our Father" (Isaiah 63:16; cf. 64:8).

Jeremiah was like a voice crying in the wilderness. Ancient Israel had no regard for the fatherhood of God, much to God's sorrow. He mourned over the people. "'How I would set you among My sons and give you a pleasant land, the most beautiful inheritance of the nations!' And I said, 'You shall call Me, My Father, and not turn away from following Me'" (Jeremiah 3:19).

There was no response. Not until the unique Son of God came into the world was the fatherhood of God truly recognized. But God still invites people to become His sons through faith in Jesus Christ. As Paul says to Christians, "You are all sons of God through faith in Christ Jesus" (Galatians 3:26).

Have you responded? If not, God is not *your* Father. He wants to be, but cannot be until you come to Him through faith in Christ Jesus. Then you, too, will be able to say:

I believe in God the *Father* . . .

Chapter Four

"I BELIEVE IN GOD THE FATHER ALMIGHTY"

I believe in God the Father *Almighty*
Maker of Heaven and Earth . . .

*T*hose who formulated the Creed added the word *Almighty* to their statement of belief in God the Father in order to distinguish between earthly fatherhood and God's fatherhood. *Almighty* means "able to do all things." The omnipotent God is able to do all things.

The New Testament states God's omnipotence in various ways. He is able to save "to the uttermost" (Hebrews 7:25 KJV). He is "able to make all grace abound" (2 Corinthians 9:8). He is "able to keep [us] from falling" (Jude 24 KJV). He is "able to build [us] up" (Acts 20:32). Finally, He is "able to do exceeding abundantly above all that we ask or think" (Ephesians 3:20 KJV).

All of these statements, even though abbreviated, demonstrate the omnipotence of God. He who is "able . . . to save . . . to the uttermost (Hebrews 7:25 KJV) is also "able to do immeasurably more than all we ask or imagine" (Ephesians 3:20 NIV). God is almighty. There is nothing He cannot do.

Believing that God is almighty is only logical. An impotent God is inconceivable. Who would worship or love a puny God? But does the almighty God care about us, His children? Yes, of course! That is implied in the name *Father.* The term *almighty* says He can do anything. The term *Father* says He *will* do all that is necessary for the well-being of His people.

We know that He is truly caring and will do what is best for us because He has said so. Furthermore, He has proved the truth of His promises. Paul explains:

> We know that God causes all things to work together for good to those who love God, to those who are called according to His purpose. For whom He foreknew, He also predestined to become conformed to the image of His Son; . . . and these whom He predestined, He also called; and these whom He called, He also justified; and these whom He justified, He also glorified. (Romans 8:28–30)

Paul then asks a rhetorical question: "If God is for us, who is against us?" (v. 31). Good question! Paul himself answers it. "He who did not spare His own Son, but delivered Him over for us all, how will He not also with Him freely give us all things?" (v. 32). God is for us.

Clearly, the Creed links the truth of God's fatherhood with the truth of His omnipotence. A father's heart moves the almighty hand. Divine power is not controlled by a cold, calculating mind, but by the heart of a warm, loving, divine Father—a caring Creator. The psalmist says, for example, "My help comes from the Lord, who made heaven and earth" (Psalm 121:2). And again, "Our help is in the name of the Lord, who made heaven and earth" (Psalm 124:8). Or take the wonderful greeting of those who guarded the temple at night: "May the Lord bless you from Zion, He who made heaven and earth" (Psalm 134:3). But perhaps the loveliest statement of God's might and love comes from Isaiah, who asks:

> Do you not know? Have you not heard? The Everlasting God, the Lord, the Creator of the ends of the earth does not become weary or tired. . . . He gives strength to the weary, and to him who lacks might He increases power. Though youths grow weary and tired, and vigorous young men stumble badly, yet those who wait for the Lord will gain new strength; they will mount up with wings like eagles, they will run and not get tired, they will walk and not become weary. (Isaiah 40:28–31)

The Creator of the ends of the earth cares dearly for His people. The power of *Almighty* God is at our service. The God who made heaven and earth is our Helper.

Science ignores the testimony of Scripture and asks only how the world was made. Various extrabiblical answers are given. Polytheism ascribes creation to many gods. Materialism says the world came into existence by chance. Deism allows for the action of a God at one time but adds that He quickly left it to its own devices. Pantheism confines God to the world He made and identifies Him with it. But the Bible teaches us that God made the world. He is imminent (He is in the world) and transcendent (He exists apart from the world and is therefore able to govern it).

The God who created and governs the world has a

father's heart. The best of earthly fathers is but a faint reflection of the Father in heaven. The world's most loving father is unloving when compared with Him. Of that Father, John said simply and beautifully, "The Father has sent the Son to be the Savior of the world" (1 John 4:14). God did not send His Son on a business trip or a vacation; He sent Him on a mission that would be full of grief and pain. If that was not love, there is not love in all the universe. But it was love, and the Father who showed it is "God the Father *Almighty*."

Chapter Five

"I BELIEVE IN JESUS CHRIST"

I believe in God the Father Almighty,
Maker of heaven and earth:
And in *Jesus Christ* ...

*J*esus Christ dominates the Apostles' Creed. The amazingly concise Creed sums up in seventy-eight words the content of Christian belief about the Triune God. Nine words refer to the Father, four to the Holy Spirit, and sixty-five to the Son. He is, as one writer expressed it, "central in the revelation of redemption ... the Focus and Fullness of the Christian religion ... the Fact and Truth which give vitality to all other facts and truths."[1]

The Creed makes seven great statements about Christ. Each statement of fact implies great truths. For example, Christ's sinlessness is implied by the fact of His conception: He "was conceived by the Holy Ghost." His intercessory work as our great High Priest is implied by the fact of His ascension. The Creed gives only the bare facts.

Look at the immediate truths *explicit* in the Creed's statement of facts. First, consider Christ's person and His relationship with the Father and with us: "His only Son, our Lord . . ." Second is His incarnation: "Who was conceived by the Holy Ghost, born of the Virgin Mary . . ." Third, look at His sufferings and death: "Suffered under Pontius Pilate, was crucified, dead and buried . . ." The reference to Pilate, death, and burial brings the Cross before our eyes.

The fourth statement refers to the realm in which Christ's spirit spent three days and three nights: "He descended into Hell . . ." Then His resurrection is proclaimed: "The third day He rose from the dead . . ." The sixth statement concerns His ascension and session: "He ascended into heaven, and sitteth on the right hand of God the Father Almighty . . ." Finally, the Creed states His return to judge the world, even as He said He would do: "From thence He shall come to judge the quick and the dead."

At least two facts are striking. First is the juxtaposition of suffering and glory. He suffered under Pilate, was crucified, died, and was buried. But He was also raised from the dead; He ascended to heaven; and in due time He will return to judge the world that rejected Him.

Second, the Creed omits any reference to Christ's life on earth. His Incarnation and vicarious death are the facts that really matter. The Incarnation tells who He was —God's sinless Son. In this fact is implied the kind of life He lived on earth and the nature of His death. The death of that Holy Person was of *necessity* vicarious—for you and for me.

If it were not, then God would not have raised Him from the dead. As Paul says, He "was delivered over because of our transgressions, and was raised because of our justification" (Romans 4:25).

Faith in Jesus distinguishes Christianity from all other faiths. Judaism and Islam are monotheistic and acknowledge Jesus as a prophet, but deny His deity and lordship. Jesus Christ was more than a mere man; He was God. He was both human and divine. Consider the following lines of evidence.

First, He was sinless. He Himself challenged His enemies to find sin in Him. "Which one of you convicts Me of sin?" He asked (John 8:46). His followers never forgot the silence of His adversaries. Later Peter wrote that He "committed no sin, nor was any deceit found in His mouth" (1 Peter 2:22, cf. Isaiah 53:9). Paul wrote that He "knew no sin" (2 Corinthians 5:21). The sinlessness of Jesus is a moral miracle that proves His uniqueness.

Second, He said He was God. His sinlessness made it impossible for Him to lie about Himself. Either He was God or considerably less than the perfect man His followers believed Him to be. His adversaries knew that He was claiming to be equal with God. In fact, His claim was the legal ground on which they condemned Him to death. When they brought Him before Pilate, demanding the death penalty, they said, "We have a law, and by that law He ought to die because He made Himself out to be the Son of God" (John 19:7; cf. John 5:17–18; 10:30–33).

Third, He had superhuman power. He could walk on water, control the winds, and raise the dead. When some of His critics witnessed the raising of Lazarus, they became believers (John 11:45).

Fourth, He accepted the worship of His followers. If

He were only a man, His approval of those who worshiped Him would have been evil (John 9:38).

The New Testament pictures one who was at the same time both human and superhuman. The beginning of Christianity as recounted in the four Gospels was built upon the perception of the man Jesus. In Acts, the apostles constantly refer to Him as "the Lord." In the epistles, He is linked with God in the salutations and benedictions. For example, Paul prays in his Ephesian letter that grace and peace may come to his readers "from God our Father and the Lord Jesus Christ" (Ephesians 1:2). In the next line he praises "the God and Father of our Lord Jesus Christ" (v. 3).

Jesus is His name; *Christ* His title. His name—which means "Savior"—tells us what He does. His title—which means "the Anointed One"—tells us that He is able to do it. Because He is God's Anointed One, He is able to save.

The name *Jesus* (Joshua-Yeshua) was fairly common. For Mary's son, it took on new meaning. The angel told her that He would "save His people from their sins" (Matthew 1:21). His name as used in the Creed has at least two significances. First, it indicates a historical fact: Jesus Christ is not a legendary figure; He actually lived on earth. Second, the name declares His mission: to "save His people from their sins." Jesus means "*Jehovah* saves."

Christ is the Greek equivalent of the Hebrew word *Messiah,* a title meaning "The Anointed One." In ancient Israel, prophets, priests, and kings were installed in office by ceremonial anointing with oil. There grew up a hope that someday someone would combine in himself the offices of prophet, priest, and king. That is called the messianic hope.

Not until Jesus came was the hope realized. After listening to Jesus, Andrew hurried off to find his brother, Peter. "We have found the Messiah," he said (John 1:41). Months later, Jesus asked Peter who he thought Jesus was. "Thou art the Christ, the Son of the living God," Peter replied (Matthew 16:16 KJV). It was a stupendous confession, yet Jesus accepted it as correct. He told Peter he was right, in effect. "Blessed are you, Simon Barjona, because flesh and blood did not reveal this to you, but My Father who is in heaven" (Matthew 16:17).

The significance of Jesus' reply cannot be exaggerated. Jesus claimed to be the fulfillment of all the ancient prophecies about the coming Messiah. He was God's Anointed One—the prophet whose coming Moses predicted, a priest greater than Aaron, the king whose throne would be eternal.

This is what we affirm when we say:

I believe ... in *Jesus Christ* ...

NOTE

1. W. Graham Scroggie, *Christ in the Creed* (The Keswick Convention, 1929), 55.

Chapter Six

"I BELIEVE IN JESUS CHRIST, HIS ONLY SON"

I believe in God the Father Almighty,
Maker of heaven and earth:
And in Jesus Christ, *His only Son* ...

*I*n one of His conversations with certain religious people, Jesus asked, "What do you think about the Christ, whose son is He?" (Matthew 22:42). The people were stumped, probably because they resisted the implications of the answer they should have given.

The complete answer is given in the Creed: Christ is God's only Son. The question asks for a definition of the relation Christ bears to God. The answer: He is God's only Son.

The first article of the Creed prepares us for this, since parenthood implies sonship. If God is Father, there must of necessity be the Son. Jesus spoke constantly of His relationship to the Father. He also said, "He who does not honor the Son does not honor the Father who sent Him" (John 5:23). That is perhaps the statement John was thinking about when he said, "Whoever denies the Son does not have the Father; the one who confesses the Son has the Father also" (1 John 2:23). Or he may have been thinking about another statement of Christ. When certain opponents questioned His parentage, He replied, "You know neither Me nor My Father; if you knew Me, you would know My Father also" (John 8:19).

At least two things must be said about Jesus' relationship to the Father as Son. First, it is eternal; second, it is unique. Jesus did not become God's Son at His birth in Bethlehem; His relationship as Son is *eternal*. The Father sent the Son, who on earth said, "Before Abraham was born, I am" (John 8:58). Passages such as Psalm 2:7, "You are My Son, today I have begotten You," refer to His resurrection, not His birth (cf. Acts 13:33). So in His birth and in His resurrection Christ is God's Son—God's eternal Son.

He is also God's unique Son. We are taught to pray, "Our Father which art in heaven" (Matthew 6:9 KJV), but He is not our Father in the same way in which He is Father to the Son. As the Bible says, God so loved the world that He gave His only begotten Son—He gave His unique Son—that whoever believes in Him should not perish, but have eternal life. He is the "only begotten," the unique Son of God.

Jesus indicated this in His command to Mary given after His resurrection. "Go to My brethren and say to them, 'I ascend to My Father and your Father, and My God and your God'" (John 20:17). God is *His* Father in a way in which He is not our Father. Jesus does not say "our" Father of Himself and others. He is God's unique

Son, and God is His Father in a way in which He can never be our Father.

Nevertheless, we are sons of God in another sense. God gives us the right to become children of God through faith. Hence, with great privilege, we call Him our Father, and we acknowledge Jesus as God's eternal Son.

Chapter Seven

"I Believe in Jesus Christ, Our Lord"

I believe in God the Father Almighty,
Maker of Heaven and earth:
And in Jesus Christ, His only Son, *our Lord* ...

$\mathcal{W}$e believe specific things about Christ. The Creed defines His relationship to God the Father as "[God's] only Son." His relationship to *us* is indicated by His name and titles: Jesus Christ, our Lord. Jesus' friends called Him "Lord," and He accepted the title. In the room where He instituted the Last Supper, He reminded them that they called Him "Teacher and Lord," and He said, "You are right, for so I am" (John 13:13).

What does the title "Lord" mean? At least two thoughts are implied. First, He is divine. Second, He is sovereign. Unbelievers resist these claims. Nevertheless, the testimony of Christ's followers is that they believed that He was God. For example, Paul says: "For to this end Christ died and lived again, that He might be Lord both of the dead and of the living" (Romans 14:9). In the same context Paul quotes the prophet Isaiah and applies Isaiah's words to Christ: "to Me every knee will bow, every tongue will swear allegiance" (Isaiah 45:23).

In his magnificent statement about Christ, Paul says:

> God highly exalted Him, and bestowed on Him the name which is above every name, so that at the name of Jesus every knee will bow, of those who are in heaven, and on earth and under the earth, and that every tongue will confess that Jesus Christ is Lord, to the glory of God the Father. (Philippians 2:9–11)

Although the Bible does not use the word *sovereign* to refer to Christ's lordship, the concept is there. This is why Christians call Christ sovereign. The word *reign* means "royal authority, dominion, sway." In its verb form it means "to govern as king or emperor." The first part of the word *sovereign* is derived from the Latin word *super,* which means "above." From it we derive our word *supreme.* Thus, *supreme* and *reign* together make up the word *sovereign.* While we may often hear the word sovereign used to refer to earthly kings and emperors, it is wrongly used because no earthly ruler is genuinely supreme. The only true sovereign is Jesus Christ. He has supreme authority. At His ascension He claimed sovereignty in these words: "All authority has been given to Me in heaven and on earth" (Matthew 28:18). On the basis of that great claim, He, the Sovereign Lord, commissioned His disciples to spread the gospel throughout the earth, making disciples of all the nations.

Although the apostle Paul was not present when Jesus claimed universal sovereignty, Paul also recognized

Jesus as supreme ruler. Paul emphasized this truth repeatedly. For example, Paul says, "[Jesus Christ] must reign until He has put all His enemies under His feet" (1 Corinthians 15:25). In another place, Paul speaks of "the power that He has even to subject all things to Himself" (Philippians 3:21).

These passages suggest what is obvious: Christ is not presently exercising supreme authority. He permits rebellion. He allows men and women to resist His will. Death (the last enemy) still claims its victim. But the New Testament teaches us that He has supreme authority and in due time will exercise it fully.

We Christians acknowledge Jesus not only as Lord, but, in the words of the Creed, as "our Lord." That suggests fellowship in the faith. I believe that Jesus is Lord; you believe that Jesus is Lord; therefore, He is our Lord. When Thomas said, "My Lord and my God!" (John 20:28), he committed himself to a fellowship in the apostolic community. And today in the Creed, we confess not only a personal belief, but also a communal belief.

Why is the possessive *our* important? Because it makes distinctions between people—those who acknowledge Jesus as Lord and those who refuse to do so. For us Christians, Jesus is Lord. It is this attitude toward Him that makes us a community of believers. Even James, the brother of Jesus, learned to call Him "our glorious Lord Jesus Christ" (James 2:1). Peter called Him "our Lord Jesus Christ" (1 Peter 1:3) and ascribed to Him "dominion forever and ever" (1 Peter 5:11).

Even within the Christian community, however, belief is very personal. John records the great scene in which doubting Thomas, face-to-face with Jesus after His resurrection, says, "My Lord and my God!" (John 20:28).

If Thomas had not made that confession, he would not have been a Christian. Paul clearly summarizes apostolic opinion and makes clear the necessity of personal confession that Jesus Christ is Lord in two passages. First, in Romans 10:9, Paul states: "If you confess with your mouth Jesus as Lord, and believe in your heart that God raised Him from the dead, you will be saved." You must confess with your mouth and believe in your heart exactly what Thomas believed: that God raised Jesus from the dead and that Jesus is Lord.

Second, in 1 Corinthians 12:3, Paul says: "No one speaking by the Spirit of God says, 'Jesus is accursed'; and no one can say, 'Jesus is Lord,' except by the Holy Spirit." That passage affirms that Jesus is Lord. Belief in Him that does not acknowledge His lordship is not good enough; it is neither biblical nor Christian. Not every person who calls himself a Christian realizes that Jesus claims to be God and is called God by His early disciples. The New Testament insists that His followers must accept Him as divine. It is not enough to believe that He was a fine man. He is Lord, or He is nothing. A fine ethical teacher may be worthy of respect, but he cannot save your soul. Only God can do that. This is precisely what Christians believe about Jesus Christ. He is Lord. He is God.

No greater confession of faith can be made than that. If you can say with sincerity, "I believe in Jesus Christ, God's only Son, our Lord," you are part of the community of genuinely Christian people. With all Christians everywhere, you also can say:

I believe in Jesus Christ, [God's] only Son, our *Lord* ...

Chapter Eight

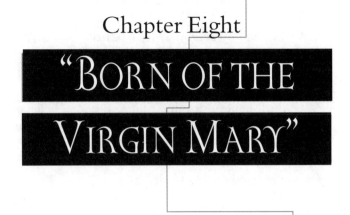

"BORN OF THE VIRGIN MARY"

... Jesus Christ, His only Son, our Lord,
Who was conceived by the Holy Ghost,
Born of the Virgin Mary ...

*O*ne of the most difficult propositions of the Christian faith is Christ's Virgin Birth. What does it mean to be "conceived by the Holy Ghost, born of the Virgin Mary"? No one has explained it better than Bishop John Pearson, whose *Expositions of the Creed* was published in 1867. His treatment of this statement of Christ's conception may be summarized in this way:

1. Christ was conceived by the operation of the Holy Spirit in the womb of the Virgin Mary.
2. Christ had no earthly father, but was only the reputed son of Joseph.
3. We cannot explain the process of His conception, that is, how the virgin conceived of or by the Holy Spirit.

4. We know, however, that Jesus Christ was made man of the substance of His mother and of no other.
5. Through her, He was descended from David and from Abraham.
6. We must believe this doctrine in order to believe in the perfect sinlessness of Him who was "the Lamb of God" and "the Second Adam."

Bishop Pearson concludes that he is

> fully assured that the Word was in this manner made flesh, that He was really and truly conceived in the womb of a woman, but not after the manner of man; not by carnal copulation, not by the common way of human propagation, but by the singular, powerful, invisible, immediate operation of the Holy Ghost, whereby a virgin was beyond the law of nature enabled to conceive, and that which was conceived in her was originally and completely sanctified.[1]

The Virgin Birth obviously was supernatural. Because it cannot be repeated, the Virgin Birth is not subject to scientific treatment in the laboratory. Hence, it must be received by faith.

That does not mean that the doctrine defies logic; it does not. Why should it be doubted that God the Father Almighty could bring His Son into the world in that way? God can do anything. He can enable a barren woman to bear children, and He can enable a virgin to conceive without the help of a man.

There are two good reasons for believing that Jesus Christ was virgin born: first, the testimony of Scripture, and second, His sinlessness. Every other human being, descended from Adam, is born with a sinful nature. Christ's nature was unblemished. He said so, and his life proved it. No other explanation is possible but His miraculous birth. Like us, He was born. Unlike us, He was born of a virgin.

"Born of the Virgin Mary" does not mean that His actual birth process was miraculous. There is no evidence that the birth was in any way exceptional. Nor does the expression mean *merely* that the conception was supernatural. At least two other Bible characters conceived supernaturally—the mothers of Isaac and John the Baptist. The phrase "born of the Virgin Mary" must always be considered in conjunction with its companion phrase "conceived by the Holy Ghost."

The Virgin Birth is not, strictly speaking, evidence for the deity of Christ. God could have ordered a virgin birth for anyone, if it would have suited His purposes. The doctrine simply explains the earthly origin of Jesus Christ. He was "conceived by the Holy Ghost, born of the Virgin Mary."

The doctrine has no recorded place in the preaching of the apostles. Why not? Probably because belief in it is possible even to those who deny a greater truth—the deity of Christ. Superstitious or merely credulous people are capable of believing in a virgin birth without acknowledging that Jesus is God's Son.

Christ's Sonship is proved by the Resurrection, not by the manner of His birth. Hence, the apostles testified to the fact of the Resurrection (cf. Romans 1:4). Those who accept the fact of Christ's resurrection have no difficulty believing that He was virgin born.

If, at the Incarnation, Jesus had entered the world as an adult instead of coming into the world as He did—a baby born of a virgin—there would have been two persons in the body He assumed. But Scripture is emphatic concerning the unity of His personality. He was not two persons; He was one person possessing two natures—the divine and the human. Theologians call the union of two natures in one personality "the hypostatic union."

What this means to us is that God has come among us in the person of Jesus Christ. This is what we proclaim when we say:

> I believe in Jesus Christ ...
> Who was conceived by the Holy Ghost,
> *Born of the Virgin Mary* ...

NOTE

1. John Pearson, *An Exposition of the Creed* (London: Bell & Daldy, 1867), 261.

Chapter Nine

"SUFFERED UNDER PONTIUS PILATE"

...Jesus Christ, His only Son, our Lord,
Who ... *suffered under Pontius Pilate* ...

*T*he Apostles' Creed jumps from Christ's birth to Christ's sufferings, omitting all reference to His life. Christ's life is not a subject for belief, but for example and emulation.

The New Testament emphasis is on His death, not His Life. Our Lord Himself explained that He was born in order to die, not to live. After the Resurrection He gently rebuked certain disciples for not knowing that His death was essential to His saving mission. "O foolish men and slow of heart to believe in all that the prophets have spoken!" He said. "Was it not necessary for the Christ to suffer these things and to enter into His glory?" (Luke 24:25–26).

The synoptic gospels—Matthew, Mark, and Luke—devote a third of their space to the account of His death.

John devotes fully half of his gospel to narrating the death of Christ. The Creed mentions neither the mental sufferings of Christ nor any of the sufferings that preceded Passion Week. In His lifetime our Lord suffered from various pressures, including anticipation of that dread hour when His Father would forsake Him. He suffered at the hands of Satan, and He suffered at the hands of evil men who sought to kill Him. Before the final events He thanked His friends for having stood by Him during His trials. The Creed mentions none of those trials.

The explanation may be that, in themselves, His sufferings had no power to save. Many of His sufferings were simply part of the human experience, intensified for Him, no doubt, by His essential holiness. His death made it possible for God to save lost people. So the Creed draws attention to His death.

Note the reference to Pontius Pilate, the Roman governor of Judea at the time of Christ's trial and execution. Why is Pilate mentioned? Bishop Pearson gives three reasons: First, in order to indicate the time of Christ's sufferings and death; second, in order to furnish us with an external testimony to Christ's death (Pilate was also a witness to the innocence of Jesus, whom he nevertheless handed over to the executioners); third, in order to confirm prophecy.

Here is Pearson's expansion of the brief statement in the Creed:

> In the fulness of time God sent His Son (who) did suffer for the sins of men, after the fifteenth year of Tiberius, the Roman Emperor, and before his death, in the time of Pontius Pilate, the Caesarian procurator of Judea, who, to

please the nation of the Jews, did condemn Him whom he pronounced innocent, and delivered Him, according to the Scriptures, to die a painful and shameful death upon the cross.[1]

Pearson's three points are well made. The Creed's reference to Pilate not only fixes the date of Christ's death, but it also emphasizes the historicity of the event. Christ's death actually took place, and the secular world is forced to confirm it. Historians such as Josephus and Tacitus agree with the Gospels that Pilate existed and that Christ suffered at his hands.

Two facts should not be overlooked. First, Pilate attested to the innocence of Jesus. "I find no fault in this man," Pilate said repeatedly. If Jesus was legally innocent of any crime, why was He condemned to death? Think about it, especially in light of Old Testament predictions that the Messiah would suffer on behalf of sinful people.

Second, Pilate contributed to the sufferings of Christ. Pilate ordered Him flogged and handed Him over to the executioners. Thus, the representative of the Roman government—the most powerful secular force on earth at the time—did despite to the Lord of glory.

The Scriptures anticipated that in various places, including the second psalm, which says, "The kings of the earth take their stand and the rulers take counsel together against the Lord and against His Anointed" (Psalm 2:2).

The same psalm tells how God laughs at the pretensions of men who think that they can so easily dispose of God's Messiah. But God is not amused; He is furious. In His fury, the psalm says, He declares His purpose for the

Messiah whom Pilate (and through him the many rulers of the world) rejected.

God is also loving. Hence, His warning:

> Worship the Lord with reverence and rejoice with trembling. Do homage to the Son, that He not become angry, and you perish in the way. For His wrath may soon be kindled. How blessed are all who take refuge in Him! (Psalm 2:11–12)

Pilate ignored the warning and invitation. How about you?

NOTE

1. John Pearson, *An Exposition of the Creed* (London: Bell & Daldy, 1867), 306–7.

Chapter Ten

"I BELIEVE IN JESUS CHRIST ... CRUCIFIED"

... Jesus Christ, His only Son, our Lord ...
Suffered under Pontius Pilate,
Was *crucified,* dead, and buried ...

*C*rucifixion was a Roman form of execution reserved for slaves and the vilest criminals. It was so shameful that Muslims, who honor Jesus as a prophet, refuse to believe He was crucified. Instead they say, "He was represented by one in His likeness."[1] For Jews, crucifixion is the greatest obstacle to belief in Jesus as the Messiah. They cannot endure the thought of a crucified Messiah. The Talmud refers to Christians as "worshipers of the hung."[2] The Romans regarded crucifixion as "most cruel," "extreme," and "infamous."[3] In the fourth century Emperor Constantine abolished it.

The Creed declares that Jesus Christ "was crucified."

We recoil from the thought. Nevertheless, He *was* crucified, and He died "according to the Scriptures" (1 Corinthians 15:3). The mode of His death, as well as the fact of His death, was predicted both in the Old Testament and by Christ Himself. For example, on the way to Jerusalem Jesus told His disciples that the chief priests and scribes would condemn Him and hand Him over to the Gentiles (that is, the Romans) to be mocked, scourged, and killed (Matthew 16:21; Mark 8:31; Luke 9:22). He amplified that statement immediately, saying that a follower must "take up his cross," a figure of speech that clearly anticipated the manner in which He would die (Matthew 16:24; Mark 8:34; Luke 9:22).

Psalm 22:16 foretells the piercing of His hands and feet. In verse 18, the psalmist says, "They divide my garments among them, and for my clothing they cast lots." Without the Cross, these lines would be either mystifying or meaningless. In the light of Christ's crucifixion, their meaning is inescapable; they anticipate the very manner of His death.

In addition to direct statements, the Old Testament also anticipates Christ's death by crucifixion in stories usually called *types.* Take the story of Abraham's being asked to sacrifice his son Isaac on an altar on Mount Moriah. As they approached the place of execution, Isaac carried the wood. In that way he foreshadowed Christ's carrying His cross (Genesis 22:6).

Christ's death by crucifixion was intimated in the story of the Exodus. Instructions were given that no bone should be broken in the lamb offered on the night of Israel's release from Egypt (Exodus 12:46). Later, John saw that as a foreshadowing of the failure of the Roman soldiers to break the legs of Jesus (John 19:33, 36; cf. Psalm 34:20).

Another type is seen in the incident of the brass (possibly bronze) snake. In a region infested by vipers, thousands of Israelites were bitten by the snakes. Moses made a brass snake and hoisted it up on a pole so that the victims could see it. As many as looked at it were healed. Our Lord referred to that when speaking of His death. "And as Moses lifted up the serpent in the wilderness," He said, "even so must the Son of Man be lifted up" (John 3:14; cf. Numbers 21:4–9). The allusion to the manner of His death is quite clear.

Crucifixion, the most painful and ignominious death imaginable, was designed to express Roman contempt for the victims. Christ's death combined maximum pain and maximum indignity. That was the way in which He was pleased to die for us—the death on the cross (Philippians 2:8).

Deuteronomy 21:23 declares that everyone who hangs on a tree is cursed, which is why the Jews find the idea of a crucified Messiah so distasteful. Yet the curse is just the point. It makes Christ's death meaningful. In Paul's words, "Christ redeemed us from the curse of the Law, having become a curse for us—for it is written, 'Cursed is everyone who hangs on a tree'" (Galatians 3:13). Thus crucifixion was theologically significant.

The manner in which Christ died has certain lessons for all of us. First, He died by hanging on a cross. He took upon Himself the curse of the law (Deuteronomy 27:26; Galatians 3:10, 13). Second, He "canceled the unfavorable record of our debts . . . by nailing it to the cross" (Colossians 2:14 TEV). Third, He gave us a picture of the way of victory over sin. As Paul says, "May it never be that I would boast, except in the cross of our Lord Jesus

Christ, through which the world has been crucified to me, and I to the world" (Galatians 6:14).

In addition to these three theological lessons from the Crucifixion, the death of Christ teaches at least two other lessons. First, the Lord gives us a lesson in dying. He who said "I am thirsty" teaches us to endure whatever may come to us (John 19:28; cf. Psalm 69:21). No dying person has ever suffered more intensely than Jesus did.

Second, His death gives us a permanent standard by which to measure our love for our brothers and sisters in the Lord and our willingness to forget self. Paul says, "The attitude [we] should have is the one that Christ Jesus had" (Philippians 2:5 TEV). What kind of attitude did He have? Paul explains that Jesus "was humble and walked the path of obedience all the way to death—his death on the cross" (Philippians 2:8 TEV). Or, as some translations have it, "even the death of the cross," as if to suggest that kind of death tested His love and willingness to serve as no other kind of death could have done (Philippians 2:7–8 TEV; cf. KJV).

Although the manner of Christ's death was important, the supremely important fact is that He died for us. As He Himself explains, the Son of Man must be lifted up, "that whoever believes will in Him have eternal life" (John 3:15). As a result, when we Christians recite the Creed we know what is implied in that single word "crucified." Hence, Paul says, "God forbid that [we] should glory, save in the cross of our Lord Jesus Christ." (Galatians 6:14 KJV).

NOTES

1. George Sales and E. M. Wherry, eds. *Comprehensive Commentary on the Qu'ran* (1896; reprint, New York: AMS), 165, 124.
2. Frederic W. Farrar, *The Life of Christ* (Philadelphia: Coates, n.d.).
3. Ibid.

Chapter Eleven

"I BELIEVE IN JESUS CHRIST ... DEAD" (1)

...Jesus Christ, His only Son, our Lord,
Was crucified, *dead,* and buried ...

*L*eon Morris points out that the Cross of Christ has profoundly influenced our language. We speak of the *crucial* point in any discussion. The word comes from the Latin word *crux,* a cross. Just as the Cross is central in Christianity, so the central point in any discussion is said to be its "crucial" point.

Two fairly well-known paintings with the same title, *The Shadow of the Cross,* illustrate the Cross's centrality. In one, the infant Jesus is running to His mother with outstretched arms. The shadow of a cross is cast by the running figure. The other painting, by Holman Hunt, shows the boy Jesus at work in His father's carpentry shop. As He stretches out His arms, His body casts the shadow of a cross.

What does the Cross mean? The Cross stands for

Christ's death. What, then, does Christ's death mean? How did He regard His death—which He fully anticipated?

Study of the various passages in which He speaks of His death yields at least two thoughts. First, He viewed His death as an act of obedience to the will of His Father, the climactic act in a life of unbroken obedience. In the Garden of Gethsemane, when Peter drew his sword to resist the men who came to take Jesus, Jesus said, "Put the sword into the sheath; the cup which the Father has given Me, shall I not drink it?" (John 18:11; cf. Matthew 26:39; John 12:27–28). The Father willed His death, and to refuse to die would be unthinkable. Second, He was a volunteer. He did not drag His feet, but willingly did His part to accomplish a plan prepared before the foundations of the earth were laid. In a magnificent passage, Paul writes:

> Although He existed in the form of God, [He] did not regard equality with God a thing to be grasped, but emptied Himself, taking the form of a bond-servant, and being made in the likeness of men. Being found in appearance as a man, He humbled Himself by becoming obedient to the point of death, even death on a cross. (Philippians 2:6–8; cf. John 10:17–18; 17:1; 19:30; Luke 24:26)

Thus, Christ's death was an act of obedience, but not the obedience of a slave forced to do what the master says. It was the obedience of one who, though equal with God, volunteered to accept the limitations of manhood in order to be able to die.

What does Christ's death mean in relation to *time?*

The answer is given in at least three passages of Scripture. First, His death was planned before time existed. As Peter says, "He was foreknown before the foundation of the world" (1 Peter 1:20). Second, Christ appeared in time in order "to put away sin by the sacrifice of Himself" (Hebrews 9:26). His death was the supreme event of all time. Finally, His death will be remembered in eternity, when time—as we know it—shall be no more. The seasons will have ended, and there will be no night there. In eternity, Christ will be served as the Lamb, a term that is forever reminiscent of His sacrificial death (Revelation 22:3).

What does Christ's death mean in relation to the universe? Was it a minor incident on a small planet? No. Christ's death had cosmic effects. Paul says, "It was the Father's good pleasure for all the fulness to dwell in [Christ], and through Him to reconcile all things to Himself, having made peace through the blood of His cross . . . whether things on earth or things in heaven" (Colossians 1:19–20). Because of Christ's death, Paul predicts that "at the name of Jesus every knee will bow, of those who are in heaven and on earth and under the earth, and that every tongue will confess that Jesus Christ is Lord, to the glory of God the Father" (Philippians 2:10–11).

Christ's death was not just an event in history. The whole universe is affected by that one death. This truth is emphasized in the epistles and in the book of Revelation.

Christ's death has determined the shape of the future. The lake of fire will receive all who refuse to acknowledge Him in their day of opportunity. The city of God has been prepared for those whose names are written in the Lamb's Book of Life. Christ's death laid the city's foundations. If He had not died, there could not have been a heaven for humankind. We praise God that He did die, and in dying created the future (Revelation 20:11–21:8; 22:3).

Chapter Twelve

"I BELIEVE IN JESUS CHRIST ... DEAD" (2)

...Jesus Christ, His only Son, our Lord,
Was crucified, *dead* ...

What did God the Father think about the death of His Son? Did He view it as a monstrous mistake, a miscarriage of justice, the murder of an innocent man?

That is a hard question, because we do not know all that God thinks. Nevertheless, we know some of God's thoughts, because He has revealed them in the Bible. The apostles, His spokesmen, suggest that Christ's death was indeed a monstrous mistake and a miscarriage of justice. For example, addressing a crowd in Jerusalem shortly after the Resurrection and Ascension, Peter said, "I know that you acted in ignorance, just as your rulers did also (Acts 3:17).

In the same message, however, Peter explained that Christ's death was the fulfillment of a plan that God had announced earlier through His prophets. Furthermore,

Peter indicated that, notwithstanding human malice, God is in control of events. "The things which God announced beforehand by the mouth of all the prophets, that His Christ should suffer, He has thus fulfilled" (Acts 3:18). God fulfilled the things He had previously announced. No matter how disordered events seemed to be, God had been in control.

That does not mean that God wrote the scenario and then moved men about like puppets on a string. As James says, "God cannot be tempted by evil, and He Himself does not tempt anyone" (James 1:13). He does not fulfill His plans by tempting or coercing men into doing what is wrong.

He fulfills His plans by bringing to power men whose inclinations lead them to do things that accomplish His purposes. When ancient Israel needed a home, God saw to it that a man of kindly disposition was Egypt's pharaoh. When it came time for the nation to leave Egypt, God allowed a monster of cruelty to occupy the throne. Each man acted freely, according to personal inclination, but each man served the purposes of God.

In the same way God allowed men like Annas and Caiaphas to control the Sanhedrin. They were evil men, jealous of their priestly and political privileges. Their decision to murder Jesus was characteristic of men like them. Responsibility for what they did rested squarely on their shoulders. Nevertheless, they accomplished the will of God. Hence in speaking of Christ's death, Peter said it happened according to divine plan. Jesus was "delivered over by the predetermined plan and foreknowledge of God" (Acts 2:23).

Clearly, Christ's death was not just a monstrous mistake or a miscarriage of justice. It was an accomplishment of extraordinary significance. By it God is now "Able . . . to save . . . to the uttermost" (Hebrews 7:25 KJV) those who come to Him through Jesus Christ, claiming the merits of His death. Christ's death secured for God a satisfactory basis for the exercise of mercy. Because Christ died, God is able to forgive without compromising His holy resistance to sin.

This truth is taught in various passages, none more profound than Paul's statement:

> God was in Christ personally reconciling the world to himself—not counting their sins against them—and has commissioned us with the message of reconciliation. We are now Christ's ambassadors, as though God were appealing direct to you through us. For Christ's sake we beg you, "Make your peace with God." For God caused Christ, who himself knew nothing of sin, actually to *be* sin for our sakes, so that in Christ we might be made good with the goodness of God. (2 Corinthians 5:19–21 PHILLIPS 1972)

This great passage asserts the deity of Christ, His sinlessness, and the vicarious character of His death.

God was not "in" Christ in the sense that He is "in" us who believe. The sentence should be punctuated to indicate that through Christ—who, though one with the Father, was nevertheless distinct from Him—God was enabled to accomplish His purpose. Thus the sentence should read, "God was, in Christ, personally reconciling the world to Himself." Paul's statement reflects Christ's claim of equality with the Father.

Paul says that Christ "knew nothing of sin" (v. 21).

He had no personal experience of sin. There were no evil thoughts in His heart, no bad words in His mouth, no wrong actions of any kind at any time. Hence, His death was vicarious, or substitutional. He was not forced to die, as we are, because of personal sin. He died for our benefit.

He died also for God's benefit, though in an entirely different sense. Christ's death gave God a satisfactory basis for exercising mercy. He can save us, not because we deserve salvation or because He decides to overlook sin, but because Christ's death satisfied the demands of God's holiness. The divine Lawgiver demands death as the penalty for sin. Christ paid the penalty.

When we say, "I believe ... in Jesus Christ ... who ... died," that is what we mean. Christ died, and as a consequence God is vindicated as a Lawgiver and also as a Savior.

The apostle John emphasizes the truth that the Father sent the Son. Why did the Father send His Son? John explains: "That we might live through Him" (1 John 4:9), "to be the propitiation for our sins" (1 John 4:10), and "to be the Savior of the world" (1 John 4:14). As John sees it, the Son could not have been a propitiation except by dying. Thus, the Father sent the Son to die.

God was not a mere bystander when Christ suffered under Pontius Pilate and was put to death. He planned it, and the objective of the plan was our salvation. As John explains, the Father sent the Son to be the Savior of the world.

What part did Satan play in the drama of Christ's death? Was Satan responsible for Christ's death? Was he pleased? The answer to these questions may be determined from several passages. First, "the Son of God appeared for this purpose, to destroy the works of the devil" (1 John 3:8).

Did He succeed in destroying the works of the devil? If so, where and when and how? Paul gives the answer:

> [Christ] has utterly wiped out the written evidence of broken commandments which always hung over our heads . . . by nailing it to the cross. And then, having drawn the sting of all the powers and authorities ranged against us, he exposed them, shattered, empty and defeated, in his own triumphant victory! (Colossians 2:14–15 PHILLIPS 1972)

The powers ranged against us were Satan and his underlings. Their power was broken at the Cross. The writer of Hebrews confirms that the Son of God became man "that through death He might render powerless him who had the power of death, that is, the devil" (Hebrews 2:14).

Christ's death was Satan's defeat. Satan is still active, to be sure. Nevertheless, he has been defeated; his power is broken, and in due time God will bind him and cast him into the lake of fire.

Our Lord knew that His suffering and death would mark Satan's defeat, and Satan probably knew it too. If so, that may explain his bitter opposition to Jesus during His lifetime and the frenzy of hatred so evident as the hour approached. When Satan perceived that he could not divert Jesus from the path to the Cross, he sought to make the path very thorny and the sufferings of death very bitter. Satan inspired the betrayal, and, no doubt, he stirred up the wrath of Jews and Gentiles alike against Jesus.

But it was Satan's last hurrah. His power was broken at the Cross. Consequently, Martin Luther could write of the triumph over Satan and sin:

> The Prince of Darkness grim—
> We tremble not for him;
> His rage we can endure,
> For lo! his doom is sure,
> One little word shall fell him.
> —Martin Luther, "A Mighty
> Fortress Is Our God"

Chapter Thirteen

THE RICHES OF
CHRIST'S DEATH

*C*hrist's death is so rich a subject that the Bible uses at least six words to explain its meaning.

First is *propitiation*. John says, God "loved us and sent His Son to be the propitiation for our sins" (1 John 4:10; cf. 2:2). Paul also used the word, though in a slightly different form: "For all have sinned and fall short of the glory of God, being justified as a gift by His grace through the redemption which is in Christ Jesus; whom God displayed publicly as a propitiation in His blood through faith" (Romans 3:23–25).

The word *propitiation* is one of a class that includes words such as reconciliation, expiation, satisfaction, and atonement. The dictionary defines the verb to *propitiate* as meaning "to appease," or "to avert the wrath and regain the favor of an offended person," and has "primary reference to the person offended." The offended person must be propitiated.

That is how it is used in the Bible. Theologians

sometimes say that the term sets forth the Godward aspect of Christ's death. "Propitiation is the work of Christ that satisfied all the claims of divine holiness, righteousness, and justice, so that God is free to act on behalf of sinners." Thus God is freed to do what He wants to do—to save sinners—but could not do without compromising His holiness. Christ's death, viewed as a propitiation, provides a righteous basis for a holy God to save sinners.

That is how Paul explains the propitiatory character of Christ's death. It demonstrates God's righteousness. It shows that God does not turn a blind eye to sin. He demanded that its penalty be paid in full, and it *was* paid in full—at the Cross. Now, having been propitiated, God is able to forgive sinners.

Christ's death provides a common meeting ground for a holy God and sinful man. God is propitiated; His character is vindicated; and sinful man receives the benefit.

The other five words used to explain the death of Christ are: *sacrifice, offering, ransom, redemption,* and *reconciliation.* The last word, *reconciliation,* has several definitions, such as "a change of relationship," "end of estrangement," and "restoration of friendship." Synonyms are *reunion* and *harmony.*

These definitions give us the general idea, but a big question remains: Who is reconciled to whom? The dictionary says that *reconciliation* (like *propitiation*) has "primary reference to the person offended." This would mean that God is reconciled. But listen to the words of Paul:

> For if while we were enemies we were reconciled to God through the death of His Son, much more, having been reconciled, we shall be saved by His life. (Romans 5:10)

> Now all these things are from God, who reconciled us to Himself through Christ and gave us the ministry of reconciliation, namely, that God was in Christ reconciling the world to Himself. (2 Corinthians 5:18–19)

The dictionary seems to be wrong. God is not reconciled; sinners are. At least one more passage must be included.

> For it was the Father's good pleasure for all the fullness to dwell in Him, and through Him to reconcile all things to Himself, having made peace through the blood of His cross. . . . And although you were formerly alienated and hostile in mind, engaged in evil deeds, yet He has now reconciled you . . . through death, in order to present you before Him holy and blameless and beyond reproach. (Colossians 1:19–22)

Several ideas emerge from a study of these passages. First, God reconciles the world to Himself by removing barriers to fellowship through the blood of Christ, in this way making people acceptable to Him. Second, God appeals to us to accept the reconciliation. Since Christ died, nothing now stands in the way. God is not only disposed to receive sinners, He can do it. Now it is up to us to seek His pardon and in this way be reconciled to Him.

Clearly, Christ's death was infinitely more than an incident in history. It was the means whereby almighty God made it possible to save sinful people without compromising His holy opposition to sin. If Christ had not offered Himself on behalf of sinful people, God could not have saved anyone without having compromised His righteousness. Another aspect of the meaning of Christ's death is indicated by the words *justify* and *justification.* From God's point of view, you and I are unjust. The death of Christ makes it possible for God to justify the unjust. Paul says that Christ's death was a demonstration of God's righteousness, "that He would be just and the justifier of the one who has faith in Jesus" (Romans 3:26).

What is justification? And how can we obtain it? The dictionary says that *justification,* as used theologically, is "being accepted by or made acceptable to God, as righteous or worthy of salvation." That is not a bad definition, except for the phrase "worthy of salvation."

Nobody is ever truly worthy, except in the sense that God views us as so intimately linked with Christ that His worthiness is transferred to us. Only in that sense can *justification* be defined in terms of worthiness.

The first part of the dictionary's definition is much better: "made acceptable to God." That is what it means to be justified before God. The emphasis is on the word *made,* which draws attention to God's work. He makes us acceptable; He justifies us.

That does not mean that God now views us as if we had never sinned. To be justified means that He knows what I am, knows what I have done in the past and will do in the future, yet He accepts me. In His official capacity of judge of all the earth He declares that I am righteous.

Those whom God justifies are not any more worthy than those whom He does not justify. All have sinned, Paul says, and all alike "fall short of the glory of God" (Romans 3:23). Each of us fails the test. But God pronounces righteous "the one who has faith in Jesus" (Romans 3:26).

How can God justify unjust people? If the problem puzzles you, be assured that you are not the first to be troubled. Thousands of years ago one of Job's friends asked the same question: "How then can a man be just with God? Or how can he be clean who is born of woman?" (Job 25:4). Job's friend implied that it could not be done. Yet Paul says it *can* be done and that God does it; He justifies the unjust (Romans 3:26). First, He provides a righteous basis for justification in the death of His Son, Jesus Christ. Second, He demands a certain response from all those whom He justifies. They must have faith in Jesus. Accordingly, God pronounces them righteous.

God does not ask for much—just faith in Jesus. Yet He did ask a lot—the death of Christ. For us, salvation is free. For God, it was costly indeed. It cost Him the Incarnation and subsequent death of His only Son.

By now it should be clear that the death of Christ is a vast subject. Nobody has sounded its depths. Nevertheless, from careful study several prominent ideas emerge. First, the death of Christ is a demonstration of God's character. Second, the death of Christ is a vindication of divine law. Christ, though personally innocent, assumed responsibility for our sins. Third, the death of Christ is the basis of divine pardon.

The meaning of this last point is explained:

[The] one who pardons really accepts the results of the wrong done to him in order that he may exempt the other from any punishment. Thus . . . when a man cancels a debt, he, of necessity, loses the amount, and if he pardons an insult or a blow, he accepts in his person the injury done in either case. So human pardon may be said to cancel at its own expense any wrong done, and this principle of the innocent suffering for the guilty is the fundamental truth of the Atonement. It is, therefore, urged with great force that every act of forgiveness is really an Act of Atonement, and thus human forgiveness, so far from obviating the necessity of Diving Atonement, really illuminates, vindicates and necessitates the Divine pardon, for "forgiveness is mercy which has first satisfied the principle of justice." It is on this ground we hold that Christ's Death made it possible for God to forgive sin. What His justice demanded His love provided. This fact of the Death of Jesus Christ as the foundation of pardon is unchallengeable in the New Testament. Repentance cannot undo the past; it can only affect the future, and any religion which does not begin with deliverance can never be a success as a discipline. Christ spoke of and dealt with the fact of deformity as well as of growth.[1]

Divine pardon, therefore, does not come cheaply. At least two things are required: The sinner must face his judge, and a suitable substitute must be found for the sinner. That is what took place at Calvary. Christ offered Himself as the sinner's substitute and represented him before God. God's wrath against sin was poured out on Christ. Since Christ assumed responsibility for the sins of every sinner who has ever lived or will live, He had to receive God's stroke.

Christ's death is the basis of our acceptance by God. At least two major passages touch on the subject. First, Ephesians 1:6: "He [that is, God] hath made us accepted in the beloved" (KJV). Or, as J. B. Phillips (1958) renders the passage, God "has made us welcome in the everlasting love he bears toward the Beloved." To be accepted is to be made welcome.

The beloved is God's Son, Jesus Christ. No doubt Paul was thinking of the baptism of Jesus, when the voice from heaven was heard, saying, "This is My beloved Son, in whom I am well-pleased" (Matthew 3:17).

Acceptance depends upon a relationship. "In the beloved" describes the relationship as union with God's beloved Son. United with Christ, we are accepted. Apart from that relationship, we have no possibility of acceptance by God. Paul uses the word *alienated* to define the position of the unforgiven—alienated from God (Colossians 1:21). Isaiah told his own people that their sins had separated them from God. God refused to hear them. They were not accepted.

In Christ, on the other hand, one is not only accepted, but he also has all the benefits that come with acceptance. Read Paul's epistle to the Ephesians and underline the words "in Christ," or "in Him." Count the benefits that are listed.

The second passage is Romans 8:33–34: "Who will bring a charge against God's elect? God is the one who justifies; who is the one who condemns? Christ Jesus is He who died, yes, rather who was raised, who is at the right hand of God, who also intercedes for us." No statement could make it plainer that acceptance is total. God Himself is on our side. Who can bring a charge against us? Not God. He is the one who justifies, and if He justifies us, who can condemn us? Is anybody greater than God?

Christ is on our side. He died for us; He was raised for us; and He now intercedes for us. Is anybody greater than He? No! We rest assured that we are now "accepted in the Beloved."

How should we respond to the death of Christ? The first response is belief. I do not mean belief in the fact of Christ's death. Even His executioners believed in the fact of His death; otherwise, they would not have given orders for the burial. Belief in His death means belief in its purpose. As Paul says, "Christ died for our sins according to the Scriptures" (1 Corinthians 15:3). Not unless one believes in His death "for our sins" and accepts it personally does that one become a Christian.

The second response is a feeling of assurance. We know that God is with us. No matter how dark the path, or how harrowing the experiences, or how deep the grief, or how intense the pain we may experience, it is nothing compared to the Cross. Why should we doubt our Father's love? God the Father "did not spare His own Son, but delivered him over for us all, how will He not also with Him freely give us all things?" (Romans 8:32).

A third response to the death of Christ should be devoted service to Him. As Paul says, "The love of Christ controls us" (2 Corinthians 5:14). He meant Christ's love for us. Our love for Him is weak and unreliable. If Christ loves us enough to die for us, how can we ignore Him or render indifferent service to Him?

The death of Christ also teaches us how to view positions of advantage. Christ did not regard equality with God a thing to be grasped tightly; He willingly surrendered it at the Incarnation. Even so, we who believe in Him should view every privilege as something to be sacrificed, if necessary.

Moreover, His willingness to become a man and to

die on the cross tells us how to measure our own obedience to the will of God. Are we also obedient, if need be, unto death?

Are we sufficiently concerned about the needs of our brothers and sisters in the Lord to suffer some loss on their behalf? This is one of the lessons of Christ's death. That magnificent passage in Philippians 2 encourages Christians to look out for the interests of others. He was willing to die for others. What are we willing to do?

> Don't be selfish; don't live to make a good impression on others. Be humble, thinking of others as better than yourself. Don't think only about your own affairs, but be interested in others, too, and what they are doing. (Philippians 2:3–4 NLT)

I believe … in Jesus Christ …
[Who] was crucified, dead, and buried …

NOTE
1. W. Griffith Thomas, *Principles of Theology* (London: Canterbury, 1930), 58.

Chapter Fourteen

"I BELIEVE IN JESUS CHRIST ... BURIED"

> ... Jesus Christ, His only Son, our Lord,
> Was crucified, dead, and *buried* ...

Was it necessary to say, "I believe Jesus Christ was buried"? Why not simply assume that He was buried and proceed to a discussion of His resurrection?

The Bible takes pains to describe Christ's burial. Each of the Gospels mentions it, and each of the evangelists adds details the others omit. For example, Matthew alone says that Joseph, who provided the tomb, was a rich man. Only Mark says that he was an honorable counselor.

The Epistles also refer to Christ's burial. In 1 Corinthians 15:3–4, Paul includes the burial in a list of the essentials of the gospel. Paul says that he delivered (i.e., preached) "as of first importance ... that Christ died for our sins according to the Scriptures, and that He was buried, and that He was raised on the third day according to the Scriptures."

Why is the account of His burials important? Two reasons may be given. First, the burial gives assurance that Christ really died. Skeptics have tried to explain belief in the resurrection by saying that Christ merely fainted—that He was not dead, and, therefore, He did not really rise from the dead; He just regained consciousness. But the Gospels make clear that He really died, that His executioners verified His death, and that Pilate, the Roman governor, gave permission to bury the body.

Second, the burial was important for its instruction in the care of dead bodies. Sometimes people carelessly say that when they are dead they don't care whether their bodies are buried or slung on the nearest rubbish heap. The Bible indicates respect for a corpse. When Stephen was martyred, devout men buried him. The body of Dorcas was washed according to the custom of the times and laid in an upper room before burial. No dead body was ever treated more tenderly than that of our Lord.

Significantly, perhaps, as Christian influence increased in the Roman Empire, cremation—widely practiced by Greeks and Romans—died out and was replaced by proper burial. Evidently Christians living in the pagan world wanted to be buried, even as their Lord was buried. For some, no doubt, it was a dramatic way of expressing their hope of resurrection.

Burial of the body intact is not necessary; in time, any body disintegrates. The man whose body was eaten by a shark will be as easily raised by the power of almighty God as the dust of one whose remains have moldered in a leaded coffin. We don't know how God will do it; knowing *who* will do it is enough.

Christ's burial was a significant part of the work He

accomplished for us in His death. What did Jesus accomplish by dying for us? Among other things, He personally absorbed God's wrath against sin. In His death sin was judged. Sin was also taken away. John the Baptist said that Jesus was "the Lamb of God who takes away the sin of the world" (John 1:29). The "taking away" of sins was typified in the Old Testament ritual of the scapegoat. The high priest laid his hands on the head of the scapegoat, confessed his sins and the sins of the people over the head of the goat, then sent the goat into the wilderness. Leviticus 16:22 explains that "the goat shall bear on itself all their iniquities to a solitary land."

Obviously, goats cannot really assume responsibility for the sins of human beings. But God wanted to portray the work of Christ in dramatic form. The scapegoat turned loose in the wilderness, too far away to return to the camp, portrayed Christ's work in "taking away" sins and corresponded to His burial. As someone has written,

> That final disposition of sin is accomplished in his burial. He went into the tomb a sin offering sacrificed unto death. He came out completely unrelated to the burden of sin. Such is the doctrinal significance of the words, "and . . . was buried." There could be no tracing of the disposition of sin achieved in the tomb as there was never tracing of the further life and existence of the scapegoat after it was released in the wilderness. In that burial which was an aspect of Christ's undertaking in behalf of the believer's sin nature, too, there is also evidently a disposition of those judgments which duly fell upon him.

If that sounds difficult, John Bunyan may help. In *The Pilgrim's Progress* he tells how the man with a burden strapped to his back eventually got rid of it. The burden symbolized his sins and consciousness of guilt. When the man ascended the hill called Calvary and contemplated the Cross, his eyes filled with tears of gratitude to the Savior who had hung there for him. "Blest be the Cross," he began to say. Then he corrected himself. "Blest rather be the Man who suffered there for me!" he shouted. And then, Bunyan says, he saw in his dream that the cords binding that heavy burden to the man's back snapped. The load went bounding down the hill and rolled into an empty tomb, and Bunyan said he never saw it again.[1]

We sometimes sing a chorus that expresses this truth:

> Living He loved me
> Dying He saved me;
> Buried, He carried my sins far away.
> —J. Wilbur Chapman, "One Day"[2]

We affirm this truth when we recognize our Lord's burial.

NOTES

1. John Bunyan, *The Pilgrim's Progress* (Philadelphia: John C. Winston, 1890), 56.
2. Copyright 1910 by C. H. Marsh. © renewed 1938, The Rodeheaver Co. (a div. of Word, Inc.). All rights reserved. Used by permission.

Chapter Fifteen

"HE DESCENDED

INTO HELL"

...Jesus Christ, His only Son, our Lord,
Was crucified, dead, and buried:
He descended into hell ...

℘he Creed has one controversial statement: "He
descended into hell." Many Chrisians do not believe that Christ's spirit actually descended into the place
of departed spirits. Furthermore, the word *hell* no longer
means what it meant when the Creed was first translated
into English.

The English word *hell* is derived from the Anglo-
Saxon word *hellan,* meaning the "unseen" or "covered"
place. A few hundred years ago it was the exact equivalent of the Hebrew word *sheol* or the Greek word *hades.*
Thus, it meant the place of all souls after death. However,
with the passage of time the word came to mean the
place of punishment for the wicked dead. Its meaning
was restricted to a place of misery. Hence, the modern

English word hell is no longer the equivalent of the biblical words *sheol* or *hades* and is inappropriate in the Apostles' Creed. At His death Christ certainly did not go to hell.

Where did He go? We don't really know, because we do not understand the pertinent passages as well as we would like to. One apparently clear passage is Acts 2:24–31, part of Peter's first sermon after the Resurrection:

> But God raised [Jesus] up again, putting an end to the agony of death, since it was impossible for Him to be held in its power. For David says of Him," …My flesh also will live in hope, because You will not abandon My soul to Hades, nor allow Your Holy One to undergo decay."

Peter interprets the psalm he quotes. He says that because David was a prophet, "he looked ahead and spoke of the resurrection of the Christ, that He was neither abandoned to Hades, nor did his flesh suffer decay" (v. 31).

The passage from the psalm is not as clear as it first appears; it does not state categorically nor necessarily imply that Christ's Spirit went to hades. Nevertheless, this is one of two or three important passages on which the creedal statement is based. Did Christ's spirit go to hades? We know where His body was—in a new tomb in a garden near where He was crucified. Where was His soul?

The Lord Himself said that He would be in paradise. When the thief who was crucified beside Him asked Jesus to remember him when He came into His kingdom, Jesus told him that he would not have to wait till then. "Today," Jesus said, "you shall be with Me in Paradise" (Luke 23:43).

Where was that paradise? Some students believe it was heaven. The word is used only twice again in the New Testament, and in each instance it seems to indicate the presence of God. For example, in Revelation the Tree of Life is said to be "in the Paradise of God" (Revelation 2:7; cf. 22:2). According to that interpretation, at death our Lord's spirit went to heaven, to await the resurrection of His body. Those who hold that view believe that is what the Lord Himself indicated when He said, "Father, into Your hands I commit My spirit" (Luke 23:46).

That interpretation is certainly possible, but it is not required by the texts cited. When Jesus committed His spirit into the Father's hand, He may have only acknowledged the Father's power to dispose of it as He willed. Moreover, in the Greek translation of the Old Testament the same word that gives us "paradise" in the New Testament is translated "garden" or "grove." For example, the Garden of Eden is a paradise,[1] an equivalent of "Abraham's bosom," a poetic term descriptive of the place of the blessed dead (Luke 16:22).

It does not matter where Jesus was during the interval between His death and resurrection. If it did, the Scriptures would have been much clearer than they appear to be. The emphasis in the Bible is not on the place where He spent the three days and three nights. The emphasis is on the truth that He did not stay there; He came back to His disciples. He was raised from the dead, even as He said He would be.

We do not have to decide whether we believe that Christ's spirit went to hades. What we must believe is that His spirit was not *abandoned* to hades. Death in all its aspects, including the disposition of both body and soul, was only temporary. Three days after His burial He emerged from the grave, body and soul intact. Scriptures in support of this great truth are unmistakably clear. If, as the Creed affirms, Jesus descended into hades, what was the significance of the descent? What does it mean?

Some suggest that in descending into hades Jesus perfected His manhood. He became one of us. He was born; He grew up; He lived; He died; His body was buried; and His spirit went into the unseen world to await resurrection. Three days later He was raised, and He ascended into heaven. Only the Resurrection and Ascension experiences were novel.

B. F. Wescott comments:

> As it stands [the doctrine that He descended into hades], completes our conception of the Lord's death. To our minds death is the separation of body and soul. According to this conception, Christ in dying shared to the full our lot. His body was laid in the tomb. His soul passed into that state in which we conceive that ours shall enter. He has won for God and hallowed every condition of human experience. We cannot be where He has not been. He bore our nature as living; He bore our nature as dead.[2]

Christ tasted every human experience, including residence in the abode of the dead. Thus, He was "made like His brethren in all things" (Hebrews 2:17). He was also different personally and in what He experienced. Because He was not a *mere* man, death could not hold Him; He arose triumphant from the grave, and He ascended to heaven.

A comparison of various passages suggests that the risen Savior released the blessed dead in hades and led them to glory (see Ephesians 4:8; Hebrews 11:40; 12:18, 23). If so, hades is no longer the abode of the blessed dead; it has been emptied of all but the wicked, who await their eternal doom. Hades has become hell.

The souls of those who receive Christ as Savior are immediately transported to heaven when they die. They do not "descend" into hades; they "ascend" to be with the Lord. When Paul was an old man in a Roman prison he wrote to his friends and said that he had a "desire to depart and be with Christ" (Philippians 1:23). For him, death meant reunion in heaven. And that would be "very much better" (v. 23).

Whether we think about these things every time we recite the Creed is doubtful. Nevertheless, these truths are implied in the great creedal statements. "I believe . . . in Jesus Christ . . . [who] *descended into hell,*" affirms belief in the changes the suffering Savior made for us by the things which He suffered.

NOTES

1. Genesis 2:8; cf. Nehemiah 3:15; Song of Solomon 4:12; see Nehemiah 2:8; Ecclesiastes 2:5; Song of Solomon 4:13 for a different Hebrew word translated "forest," "parks," and "orchard."
2. B. F. Wescott, *The Historic Faith* (London: Macmillan, 1885), 76–77.

Chapter Sixteen

"THE THIRD DAY HE ROSE FROM THE DEAD"

He descended into hell;
The third day *He rose from the dead* . . .

What do we mean when we say, "The third day He rose from the dead"? Creeds and confessions written much later than the Apostles' Creed expanded the statement for more precision. For example, Article IV of the Thirty-nine Articles of the Church of England expresses it in this way: "Christ did truly rise again from death, and took again His body, with flesh, bones, and all things pertaining to the perfection of man's nature."

The article emphasizes three great truths: first, the fact of the Resurrection ("Christ did truly rise again from the dead"); second, the identity of the risen body (He "took again His body"); third, the change in the risen body (He "took again His body, with flesh, bones, and all things pertaining to the perfection of man's nature").

Did you notice the omission of the word *blood?* Christ's resurrection was not resuscitation; it was a genuine resurrection. His resurrection was unlike that of Lazarus or any other person who returned to life.

How important is the truth of Christ's resurrection? In H. E. Brunner's view, "On the resurrection everything else depends."[1] Floyd Filson says, "The entire New Testament was written in the light of the resurrection."[2] These are strong statements, but no knowledgeable person would contradict them.

Paul's estimate of the importance of the Resurrection fact is clear from the various statements. Take his summary of the gospel in 1 Corinthians 15:3–4: "For I delivered to you as of first importance what I also received, that Christ died for our sins according to the Scriptures, and that He was buried, and that He was raised on the third day according to the Scriptures." Paul then lists occasions on which the Lord appeared to His followers, including all the apostles and Paul himself, and says, "Whether then it was I or they, so we preach and so you believed" (vv. 1–11). His meaning is clear: All the apostles preached that Christ had risen from the dead. In another place, Paul says, "If you confess with your mouth Jesus as Lord, and believe in your heart that God raised Him from the dead, you will be saved" (Romans 10:9). The two passages combined reveal the importance of the truth that Christ was raised from the dead. All the apostles believed it happened. They also drew a vital, unavoidable conclusion: belief in the Resurrection is necessary to salvation.

Among the evidences supporting belief in the Resurrection is the life and character of Jesus. An undeniably truthful man, Jesus clearly predicted His resurrection. If He did not rise, what does that say about His veracity?

Another evidence is the empty tomb and disappearance of the body. There are only two alternatives: either He was raised from the dead, as His disciples said He was, or the body was taken by human hands. If the body was taken, who took it? His enemies? If they took it, why did they not produce it when the apostles began to tell everybody that Jesus was alive?

Did the disciples take it? How could they have taken it? It lay behind a massive stone, officially sealed and guarded by a squad of soldiers. And would the disciples have given their lives, as many of them did, in defense of a message that was patently untrue?

The truth is, the disciples were totally unprepared for the resurrection of Christ, even though He had prophesied it. The women planned to embalm Jesus' body, expecting a corpse and not a resurrection. Many were reluctant to believe, even when faced with increasing evidence that He had risen. Their change of heart powerfully supports the fact of the Resurrection. Even unbelievers admit that the disciples believed in the Resurrection. Clearly, the disciples did not steal the body.

Ultimately, no unbelieving critic has ever successfully solved the problem of the empty tomb and the missing body. The silence of Christ's enemies is as significant as the testimony of His friends.

Paul's conversion is another powerful proof of the Resurrection. Nobody was less disposed to believe than the proud persecutor of the early church. A man of intellect and learning, he was thoroughly hostile to the name of Jesus. Yet he became a follower. In his replies to those who questioned him, Paul invariably mentioned his experience on the road to Damascus, when the risen Lord appeared to him. That experience changed Paul's life. Before King Agrippa, he told the story of his conversion, and when he came to the point about the Resurrection, Festus interrupted him. "Paul, you are out of your mind!" he said. "Your great learning is driving you mad" (Acts 26:24).

Paul's reply is significant. "I am not out of my mind, most excellent Festus," he said, "but I utter words of sober truth." Then Paul called on King Agrippa to testify that he had already heard about Christ's resurrection. "This has not been done in a corner," Paul said (vv. 25–26).

Perhaps no line of evidence is more convincing to us than the effect of Christ's appearances on His disciples. We have the record in the Gospels. However, the appearances themselves—not the record in the Gospels—accounted for early belief in the Resurrection. Here is what James Denny says:

> The narratives of the Evangelists are quite the least important part of the evidence with which we have to deal. It is no exaggeration to say that if we do not accept the resurrection on grounds which lie outside this area, we shall not accept it on the grounds presented here. The real historical evidence for the resurrection is the fact that it was believed, preached, and propagated, and produced its fruit and effect in the new phenomenon of the Christian Church, long before any of our Gospels was written. This is not said to disparage any of the Gospels, or to depreciate what they tell, but only to put the question on its true basis. Faith in the resurrection was not only preva-

lent, but immensely powerful before any of our New Testament books were written.[3]

There were two sets of appearances, one in Jerusalem, and the other in Galilee. The accounts bear the unmistakable marks of reality.

In a little volume titled *Christianity Is Christ,* W. Griffith Thomas sums up the various lines of evidence in support of the resurrection of Christ:

> Taking [the various lines of proof] singly, they must be admitted to be strong, but taking them together, the argument is cumulative and sufficient, if not overwhelming ... the resurrection is the rock from which all the hammers of criticism have never chipped a single fragment.[4]

The overwhelming evidence in support of the Resurrection has never been successfully refuted. Consequently, those who refuse to believe usually defend their unbelief by declaring that miracles do not happen.

We Christians believe that Jesus did rise from the dead. Though speaking in unison, when we recite the Creed, each of us expresses a personal belief in the Resurrection.

NOTES

1. H. E. Brunner, *Letter to the Romans,* rev. ed. (Philadelphia: Westminster, n.d.), 131.
2. Floyd V. Filson, *Jesus Christ: The Risen Lord* (Nashville: Abingdon, n.d.), 31.
3. James Denny, *Jesus and the Gospel* (New York: Gordon, 1977), 111.
4. W. Griffith Thomas, *Christianity Is Christ* (Chicago: Moody, 1965), 31.

Chapter Seventeen

"HE ASCENDED
INTO HEAVEN"

The third day He rose from the dead;
He ascended into heaven . . .

*A*fter His resurrection Jesus Christ ascended into heaven. The Creed omits His appearances to His disciples. Defense of its statements is not the purpose of a creed. Hence, the Creed says simply that Jesus Christ ascended into heaven.

Between Passover, when our Lord was crucified, and Pentecost, after He ascended, were fifty days. (In some churches the terms *Easter* and *Whitsun,* or *Whitsunday,* are substituted for the biblical words *Passover* and *Pentecost.*) Luke says that our Lord "presented Himself alive, after His suffering, by many convincing proofs, appearing to [the disciples] over a period of forty days" (Acts 1:3). Hence, Bible students conclude that our Lord ascended to heaven forty days after the Resurrection and a few days before the holiday called Pentecost.

Why did He wait forty days? At least two explanations have been suggested: First, the number *forty* is frequently used in Scripture and usually signifies "probation," or "testing." An example is Israel's forty years in the wilderness. Second, the forty days after the Resurrection correspond to the forty days of testing by Satan. At the beginning of His public life He was tested under pressure from Satan for forty days. At the end of His life on earth He triumphed for forty days.

We do not know what He did during those forty days, unless the recorded appearances were merely a few of many. But this much is clear—the Resurrection changed the conditions of His existence. Before the Cross, He suffered self-imposed limitations such as hunger, thirst, fatigue, and sorrow in anticipating the Cross. After the Resurrection, all was changed. Canon T. C. Hammond explains:

> It seems best to regard the evidence as teaching that our Lord entered into a new existence both in Body and Spirit, but was capable of resuming such necessary relations to our present conditions as afforded unmistakable evidence of an actual resurrection without fully binding Him by the conditions of His previous humiliation. . . . The "appearance" was a gracious condescension to our need of "many proofs."[1]

Jesus spent the last day of His life on earth with His disciples in Jerusalem. They left the city together, crossed the brook Kidron, passed by Gethsemane, ascended the ridge called the Mount of Olives, and continued east toward Bethany. They chatted for a while; then He lifted up His hands to bless them. And while He was blessing them, He was lifted up. Luke says that "a cloud received Him out of their sight" (Acts 1:9). While they gazed intently at the cloud, two men in white clothing assured them that He would return "in just the same way" they had seen Him depart (vv. 10–11).

The simplicity of the account is astonishing. No embellishments are added, and no attempt is made to convince the doubtful. The disciples tell what they *saw*. Nobody saw Christ's resurrection; the disciples saw only its effects—the risen, living Lord. But they saw the actual Ascension—and not its effects. They knew what He would do in heaven, because He told them either directly or through the Holy Spirit.

The writer of Hebrews explains what happened. First, Christ "passed through the heavens" (Hebrews 4:14), and second, He entered "into heaven itself" (9:24). The first statement probably means that Christ transcended limitations of space and appeared among the eternal realities. Thus, the objections of those who quibble that heaven cannot be "out there," or "up there" are invalid. The Bible of necessity speaks of heaven as "up," since no other direction would make sense to earth-bound individuals.

The second statement, that Christ entered "into heaven itself," assures us that heaven, the abode of God, does exist. True, the Bible speaks of God's omnipresence. As Solomon said, "Heaven and the highest heaven cannot contain [Him]" (1 Kings 8:27). Nevertheless, the Bible also speaks of heaven as God's "dwelling place" (v. 43). Heaven is not an idea, a dream, or an illusion. It is a place, and Jesus is there. He passed through the heavens (that is, space), and He entered into heaven. There, in the very presence of God, He appears on our behalf (Hebrews 9:24). No wonder Paul says, "Who is the one who condemns? Christ Jesus is He who died, yes, rather who was raised, who is at the right hand of God, who also intercedes for us" (Romans 8:34).

The Apostles' Creed gives as much space to the Ascension as to the other facts of the faith, such as Christ's death and resurrection. The men who framed the Creed obviously believed the Ascension is important.

Scripture makes clear that the Ascension is important. In fact, one major portion of the New Testament—the epistle to the Hebrews—is written from the point of view of the ascended Christ. Hebrews does not mention the Resurrection. As W. Griffith Thomas comments, "It was at the Ascension that our Lord entered upon His work as Priest and King, and this is why the doctrinal position of the Epistle to the Hebrews centers in the fact of the Ascension in relation to our Lord's priesthood."[2]

John's gospel gives at least twelve references to the Ascension. John records our Lord's words of assurance to His friends: "It is to your advantage that I go away" (John 16:7; cf. 1:51; 3:13; 17:11; 20:17). At the time, they did not understand what He was saying. Later they did, and their writings reflect their agreement that the Ascension was indeed for their good.

Several advantages are apparent. First, it was a cause of real joy. Our Lord said: "You heard that I said to you, 'I go away, and I will come to you.' If you loved Me, you would have rejoiced, because I go to the Father" (John 14:28). And they did rejoice. Luke says that when He parted from them (at the Ascension), "they . . . returned to Jerusalem with great joy" (Luke 24:52). They rejoiced because they knew He was alive, and also because of His promise to come for them. Evidently the apostles and early Christians believed Jesus would return for them before they died.

The Ascension also inspired a stronger faith, making it possible for the disciples to hold fast to God in the face of adversity. As Paul says, probably quoting a Christian hymn popular at the time, "If we endure, we will also reign with Him" (2 Timothy 2:12). The connection between Christ's reign and the Ascension is unmistakable. The writer to the Hebrews urges his readers to "hold fast our confession," because "we have a great high priest who has passed through the heavens, Jesus the Son of God" (Hebrews 4:14).

Apart from the Ascension, Christ's resurrection would be considerably less meaningful than it is. In his first sermon Peter begins with the Resurrection and concludes with the Ascension. "This Jesus God raised up again, to which we are all witnesses. Therefore having been exalted to the right hand of God, and having received from the Father the promise of the Holy Spirit, He has poured forth this which you both see and hear" (Acts 2:32–33). He was raised from the dead, and He was taken up to heaven. The two events are inseparable.

As our risen and ascended Lord, Christ is far more active on our behalf than if He had not returned to heaven. Think about it this way: if He had not ascended, where would He be, and what would He be doing?

If He had not been taken up, His presence would have remained localized—sometimes in Jerusalem, sometimes somewhere else, but never in every place at the same time. Risen from the dead, about to depart for heaven, He said, "Lo, I am with you always" (Matthew 28:20). The ascended Christ promises to be with every company of believers who meet in His name, even in twos and threes (18:20).

If He had not been taken up, He would not have sent the Holy Spirit or given gifts to the church. It was the ascended Lord who sent the Holy Spirit and "gave gifts to his people" (Ephesians 4:8–12 NLT; see also Acts 2:32–33).

Suppose He had not ascended. Could He have become our great high priest? On earth, He was God's spokesman. But He was not a priest. In fact, in the epistle to the Hebrews, it says plainly, "If He were on earth, He would not be a priest at all" (Hebrews 8:4). Not until He entered into heaven itself, to appear on our behalf in the very presence of God, did He become a priest (9:24).

We need a priest; the epistle to the Hebrews makes that plain. Not an earthly priest, beset with the same sins and weaknesses that trouble the rest of us, but a heavenly priest who, having offered Himself as a sacrifice for our sins, is now able to intercede for us. He could not have become our great High Priest if He had not *ascended into heaven*.

NOTES

1. T. C. Hammond, *Reasoning Faith* (London: Inter-Varsity, 1946).
2. W. Griffith Thomas, *Principles of Theology* (London: Canterbury, 1930), 82.

Chapter Eighteen

"AND SITTETH ON THE
RIGHT HAND OF GOD"

He ascended into heaven,
And *sitteth on the right hand
of God the Father Almighty . . .*

The line that begins with Christ's ascension ends in this way: "And sitteth on the right hand of God the Father Almighty." These words express belief in the role Christ now fills in heaven. Theologians often term this His "session." The word may be archaic, though we still speak of courts in session, meaning that the judge is seated at the bench and the proceedings are under way.

Our use of the word *session* is closely related to its secular use. The Creed calls attention to the truth that our risen Savior is not just up there, having returned and doing nothing but twiddling his thumbs; rather, He is seated on the right hand of God the Father Almighty.

The central truth in the epistle to the Hebrews is that "we have . . . a high priest, who has taken His seat at the right hand of the throne of the Majesty in the heavens" (Hebrews 8:1). The High Priest is seated, that is, *in session.* But there is another idea associated with the word seated: it refers to His having finished the atoning aspect of His work. In the tabernacle, and later, the temple, there were no chairs. The blood of bulls and goats could never take away sins. Thus, sacrifices were offered repeatedly. The priests' work was never finished; they could not sit down. In contrast, by virtue of the sacrifice of Himself, which put an end to the sacrificial system, Christ is now seated.

Still, the principle idea of *session* is his work as the ascended Lord. We usually speak of Christ's work in heaven as intercession on our behalf. But there is more to His work than simple intercession. One could easily compile an impressive list of things the ascended Lord either did or does for His people. For example, He sent the Holy Spirit on the day of Pentecost (Acts 2:4); He added disciples to the church (v. 47); He healed a lame man (3:16); He appeared to Saul of Tarsus (Acts 9:1–6); He still "[comes] to the aid of those who are tempted" (Hebrews 2:18); He functions as our great High Priest, appearing in the presence of God for us (7:26); He is our Advocate (1 John 2:1); He is waiting patiently until all opposition to Him is overcome (Hebrews 10:13).

The ascended Lord did, and continues to do, much more. Biblical teaching about the *session* may be summed up thus: First, He entered into glory, where He is recognized as Lord. Then He gave—and continues to give—the Holy Spirit to every believer and gifts to the church. Finally, He assumed His priestly functions. These constitute His unfinished work—the things He is doing and will continue to do until the church is caught up (see Ephesians 4:8; 1 Thessalonians 4:17; Hebrews 2:9; 1 Peter 1:21; 3:22).

Is all that implied in the creedal statement "He … sitteth on the right hand of God the Father Almighty"? Yes—all that, and even more. Christ's presence at the Father's right hand (a metaphor) should inspire us to "keep seeking the things above, where Christ is" (Colossians 3:1). His presence there assures us that purification for sins has been made; *that* work is finished (Hebrews 7:3; 8:1; 10:12). Consequently, we believers are invited into the very presence of God. "Let us draw near," Paul says, "with a sincere heart in full assurance of faith" (Hebrews 10:22). God's arms are opened wide.

Chapter Nineteen

"FROM THENCE HE SHALL COME"

He ascended into heaven,
And sitteth on the right hand
of God the Father Almighty;
From thence He shall come
to judge the quick and the dead ...

The words "He shall come" summarize a major Bible doctrine. A creed lacking affirmation of belief in Christ's return would be incomplete and not truly Christian.

The New Testament makes some three hundred references to Christ's return—about one in every thirteen verses. Bible students have tabulated the references to various themes in order to illustrate the prominence of the theme of the Lord's return, as compared with other doctrines.

Baptism is mentioned nineteen times in seven Epistles. Fourteen Epistles do not mention the subject. The

Lord's Supper is mentioned clearly only three or four times. Twenty Epistles do not speak of it at all. The Lord's Second Coming, on the other hand, is alluded to about once in every thirteen verses in the New Testament, once in every ten verses in the Epistles.

With this evidence before us, can we overstate the importance of the truth that He will come again? Hardly! Christ's return is so clearly stated in the Bible that it is an article of faith among Christians who take their Bibles seriously. The Bible does not say flatly that you must believe in Christ's return in order to become a Christian. However, it seems reasonable to infer that refusal to believe in an event that Christ so plainly said would happen precludes any real faith in Him and in His words—without which no one can be saved. Jesus said, "He who rejects Me and does not receive My sayings, has one who judges him; the word I spoke is what will judge him at the last day" (John 12:48).

Christians agree that our Lord clearly predicted His return. This is why belief in this blessed hope is plainly stated in the Apostles' Creed and later creeds. Disagreement centers on details about His coming that are not so plainly stated, such as the time of Christ's return. But the creedal statement of belief in His return is not controversial; it says simply, "He shall come again," without attempting to work out details.

Our Lord's coming is literal and should not be confused with a spiritual "coming," such as the indwelling of Christians by the Holy Spirit. Jesus Himself said, "I will come again" (John 14:3), and at the Ascension two angels told the watching disciples that He would return "in just the same way" as He had left them (Acts 1:11). Christians in the first century were taught by the apostles to watch and wait for a literal return (see 1 Thessalonians 1:8–10).

This is the Christian's hope. We are not waiting for death, though we may die; nor for a spiritual experience, though we may have spiritual experiences. We are waiting for God's Son from heaven. As Paul explained, we are "looking for the blessed hope and the appearing of the glory of our great God and Savior, Christ Jesus" (Titus 2:13).

The Bible is unmistakably clear about the fact of Christ's return, but not as clear about its timing. Accordingly, earnest Bible students disagree in their interpretations. Some students get so enamored of their system, or so defensive in their attitude toward those who hold other views, that they run the risk of forfeiting blessings that belief in Christ's return should give them. The truth is intended to inspire and uplift Christians. How sad, then, when believers get mired in controversy over details.

At least two intended blessings may be cited. First, the blessed hope brings comfort. Jesus said, "Do not let your heart be troubled; believe in God, believe also in Me . . . I go to prepare a place for you. If I go . . . I will come again and receive you to Myself" (John 14:1–3).

The second intended blessing is godly living. The hope of Christ's return is an incentive to holiness. Speaking of the prospect that Christ will come again and that we shall see Him and be like Him, John says, "Everyone who has this hope fixed on Him purifies himself, just as He is pure" (1 John 3:3). The meaning is obvious: if we really believe that Jesus is coming again, we will live accordingly, as men and women who refuse to participate in evil.

That is what we mean when we say that He will come again.

Chapter Twenty

"TO JUDGE THE QUICK AND THE DEAD"

He ascended into heaven,
And sitteth on the right hand
of God the Father Almighty;
From thence He shall come
to judge the quick and the dead ...

*B*eginning with the Apostles' Creed, which dates back to the fourth century, all the major creeds of Christendom express belief in the eventual return of Christ. What will He do when He comes again? The Apostles' Creed states simply, "He shall come [back] to judge the quick [the living] and the dead."

Taken as it stands, the creedal statement seems to say that judgment is the only purpose in Christ's return. However, the Creed is very concise; every line implies more than appears on the surface. Judgment is not the only reason for Christ's return.

Consider the following purposes in the Second

Coming. First, He will receive all His followers to Himself. In order to do so, He will raise the bodies of those whose souls are already in heaven, and He will change the bodies of believers living at the time of the great event. It will be a "judgment" in the sense that He will reverse forever the effects of sin on the human body and human personality (1 Corinthians 15:51–58).

Second, Christ will fulfill all the promises of God made to the Jewish race. Some believe that promises made to Israel are *spiritually* fulfilled in the benefits Christians receive. But major passages, such as Romans 11, argue that these ancient promises will be *literally* fulfilled at the return of Christ (cf. Isaiah 60). God will judge Israel for its unbelief and rejection of its true Messiah (Matthew 19:28).

A third purpose for His return is to put an end to the world system itself. Peter says that when the time comes, "the earth and its works will be burned up" (2 Peter 3:10). The universe itself will be destroyed to make room for the creation of new heavens and a new earth, "in which righteousness dwells" (vv. 10–13; cf. Hebrews 1:10–12). God will remake everything—not as one who remodels an old ruin, but as one who creates something entirely new. Conceivably, the molecular structure of the new creation will be different from the system now prevailing.

Finally, Christ will return in order to destroy Satan and end the reign of death. Even before the final judgment of lost souls, Satan will have been thrown into the lake of fire, never again to trouble the inhabitants of the earth. And then the last enemy, death itself, will be abolished. John, who saw the new holy city in a vision, writes that God "will wipe away every tear from their eyes; and there will no longer be any death; there will no longer be any mourning, or crying, or pain; the first things have passed away" (Revelation 21:4; cf. 1 Corinthians 15:26, 51–57; Revelation 20:10; 21:3).

The Creed's statement that Christ will come again to judge the living and the dead summarizes several truths about judgment. First, Christ is more than a Savior; He is also a Judge. The Father, He said, has given the Son "authority to execute judgment" (John 5:27). Later, Paul said that "God will judge the secrets of men through Christ Jesus" (Romans 2:16; cf. Acts 17:31).

Nobody likes the idea of judgment, but nearly everybody acknowledges its rightness. Conscience itself demands it. Paul says that even the Gentiles who do not know the Ten Commandments "show the work of the Law written in their hearts, their conscience bearing witness and their thoughts alternately accusing or else defending them" (Romans 2:15). When Paul spoke to a Roman official (Felix) about judgment to come, the man trembled. His conscience confirmed the appropriateness of judgment and warned him that he was unprepared (Acts 24:25).

The second truth the Creed implies is that the Bible distinguishes between classes. It does not lump everyone together in one big, final judgment. The phrase "the quick and the dead" may be interpreted in two ways, according to biblical teaching. One view is that Christ will come to judge those who are living when He comes and those who have died. But the same words may be used to distinguish between those who are spiritually alive and those who, though physically alive, are nevertheless spiritually dead. Both interpretations are correct, and both are used in the Bible. The first is obvious: there are living people, and there are dead people whose remains are buried somewhere. The second interpretation is justified by passages such as Ephesians 2:1, in which unconverted people are described as "dead in . . . trespasses and sins." At conversion God makes us "alive" together with Christ.

When He comes, Christ will judge both Christians and non-Christians. He will appraise the lives of Christians and bestow rewards. For Christians, eternal life is not the issue; that was settled forever the moment we first trusted Jesus Christ as our Savior.

Judgment for non-Christians will be solemn indeed. Jesus Christ said He would come again to *judge the world*. Paul believed it. Paul told the philosophers of Athens that God "has fixed a day in which He will judge the world in righteousness through a Man whom He has appointed" (Acts 17:31). Who is the Man appointed to execute judgment? Christ, of course—the Man whom God raised from the dead.

When Paul says that God will judge the world "in righteousness," he draws attention to the principles by which God will manage the trial, so to speak. The first is God's righteousness. Paul speaks of the "righteous judgment" of God, and he also says that the Lord is the *righteous* Judge (2 Thessalonians 1:5–6; 2 Timothy 4:1; Revelation 16:5–7). In heaven angels and saved people alike praise God because His judgments are righteous (Revelation 19:1–2). There is no unfairness in them.

Abraham knew that God's judgment on Sodom would be right. "Far be it from You . . . to slay the righteous with the wicked, so that the righteous and the wicked are treated alike," Abraham said. Then he questioned what he knew to be unquestionable truth: "Shall not the Judge of all the earth deal justly?" (Genesis 18:25).

God makes allowances for varying degrees of privilege, opportunity, and responsibility. The Judge Himself, Christ, said that it would be more tolerable for the depraved cities of Tyre and Sidon in the day of judgment than for the men of Capernaum, who saw many of His miracles (Matthew 11:22–23).

Paul says that it is just for God to deal out retribution "to those who do not know God and to those who do not obey the gospel of our Lord Jesus. These will pay the penalty of eternal destruction, away from the presence of the Lord and from the glory of His power" (2 Thessalonians 1:8–9).

Passages such as this frequently evoke questions about the fate of those who have not heard the gospel. Those who ask are sometimes unbelievers who should be concerned about themselves. Believers also are concerned about those who have not heard the gospel. Two lines of thought may suggest answers. First, we will not know until the judgment day how God will deal with the heathen, but we know now how He will treat those who hear the gospel and refuse to obey it.

Second, as for those who have not heard the gospel, all *we* need to know is that their destiny is in the hands of their Creator, who is infinitely more just than we could be. He sent His Son to die for each of them—proof enough for any reasonable man that God loves him. We can trust the Judge of the earth to do what is right, for God is both holy and loving.

Meanwhile, the prospect of judgment is sobering. In his last letter, Paul evoked the specter of judgment. "I solemnly charge you in the presence of God," he said, "and of Christ Jesus, who is to judge the living and the dead, and by His appearing and His kingdom" (2 Timothy 4:1).

That verse, as the source of our creedal statement, reminds us of the particular judgment we all face when our Lord returns.

Chapter Twenty-One

"I BELIEVE IN THE HOLY GHOST"

I believe in the Holy Ghost:
The holy catholic church,
The communion of saints ...

The third part of the Creed states our Christian belief in the third Person of the Godhead, the Holy Spirit. In the Apostles' Creed, the term is "Holy Ghost," but *ghost* is an Anglo-Saxon word, now considered archaic. *Holy Spirit* is correct. At first glance all the third part of the Creed seems to say is that we believe in the Holy Spirit and in five other points of doctrine. However, there is more: the listing of five blessings immediately after the statement of belief in the Holy Spirit reminds us that the blessings are brought to us by the Holy Spirit of God.

Reference to the Holy Spirit reminds us that in the Creed we affirm our belief in the triune God—God the Father Almighty, Jesus Christ His only Son, and the Holy

Spirit. We see that the Creed is entirely biblical. It reflects many passages in Scripture but perhaps none more clearly than the great benediction of 2 Corinthians 13:14: "The grace of the Lord Jesus Christ, and the love of God, and the fellowship of the Holy Spirit, be with you all."

What do we mean when we say we believe in the Holy Spirit? We mean that the Bible teaches that the Holy Spirit is God. The Nicene Creed, which is nearly as old as the Apostles' Creed, explains that the Holy Spirit is "the Lord; the Giver of Life, proceeding from the Father and the Son, Who with the Father and the Son together is worshipped and glorified, Who spoke by the prophets."

The Holy Spirit is mentioned as early as the second verse in the Bible. At creation, "the Spirit of God was moving over the surface of the waters" (Genesis 1:2).

New Testament teaching about the Holy Spirit begins with the angel's annunciation to Mary. In reply to Mary's question about her pregnancy, the angel said that the Holy Spirit would come upon her, and the power of the Most High would overshadow her (Luke 1:34–35). The conception would be the work of God's Holy Spirit.

Living in Jerusalem at that time was an old man named Simeon. The Bible says that the Holy Spirit had told him that he would not die until he had seen the Messiah (i.e., the Christ). After the birth of Christ, the Holy Spirit prompted Simeon to go to the temple at the very time Joseph and Mary were entering the temple, with the holy infant. Thus, their paths converged, and the Holy Spirit's promise to Simeon was fulfilled; Simeon saw the Lord's Christ (Luke 2:25–27).

During Christ's life the Holy Spirit stayed in the background, so to speak. The second person of the Godhead was prominent. But as the hour of His departure drew near, our Lord prepared His disciples to respond to the work of God the Holy Spirit. In the Upper Room discourses the Lord told them that the Holy Spirit would come from God, would teach them all things, and would convict the world of sin (John 16:7–15).

As He prepared to leave His disciples, our Lord linked the Holy Spirit with the Father and the Son in the baptismal formula. "Go therefore and make disciples of all the nations," He said, "baptizing them in the name of the Father and the Son and the Holy Spirit" (Matthew 28:19).

In the New Testament the Holy Spirit is called both *God* and the *Lord* (2 Corinthians 3:18). Ananias and Sapphira learned the hard way that the Holy Spirit is God. Peter asked them why they had lied to the Holy Spirit; then he told them that they had lied to God (Acts 5:3–4).

The Holy Spirit makes God real to us. None of us was present when God created the world, nor when Christ was born. Nevertheless, Christ is real to us because the Holy Spirit reveals Him to us, even as He applies to our souls all the benefits of redemption. If it were not for the Holy Spirit, none of us could become believers: there would be no new birth, no forgiveness of sins, no founding of the church, and no fellowship of the saints (John 3:6–8; Ephesians 2:10, 22; 4:30).

All the blessings listed after the statement of belief in the Holy Ghost are bestowed upon us by the Holy Spirit of God. Take the first one: membership in "the holy catholic church." The Holy Spirit unites us to Christ, thereby making us members of His body, which is the church (1 Corinthians 12:13; Ephesians 1:22–23).

The Creed also expresses belief in the communion of saints, which means the fellowship of Christian people. By indwelling each Christian, the Holy Spirit unites us to each other. Thus, we are one in Christ. The great apostolic benediction includes reference to "the fellowship of the Holy Spirit" (2 Corinthians 13:14; Philippians 2:1).

Paul says plainly that the resurrection of the body will be accomplished by the power of the Holy Spirit. "But if the Spirit of Him who raised Jesus from the dead dwells in you, He who raised Christ Jesus from the dead will also give life to your mortal bodies through His Spirit who indwells you" (Romans 8:11).

It begins to be clear to us why the framers of the Apostles' Creed set it up as they did. Before declaring belief in the distinctive blessings of Christianity, we express our belief in the divine Person who makes those things realities. We believe in the *Holy Spirit,* who makes God real to us.

Chapter Twenty-Two

"THE HOLY CATHOLIC CHURCH"

I believe in the Holy Ghost:
The holy *catholic* church ...

*M*any Protestant believers feel uncomfortable saying, "I believe in the holy catholic church," lest use of *catholic* be interpreted as synonymous with *Roman Catholic.*

As used in the Creed, the term *catholic* does not mean Roman Catholic. The English word is the almost exact equivalent of a Greek adjective that means "universal." The word originally indicated the geographical extension of Christianity throughout the then-known world. Later on, says one authority, "came the thought of doctrinal purity and fulness, as seen in the phrase, 'catholic faith,' i.e., that which is believed everywhere and by all Christians."[1]

The church includes all true Christians in all times and in all places. Thus, its catholicity, or universality, is not only geographical. It includes all who are united to Christ since the founding of the church, shortly after His ascension. Obviously, we do not mean a local church, or any particular denomination, no matter how impressive the denomination may be. No denomination in Christendom includes in its membership all the Christians on earth at the present time, much less those of all times.

The universal aspect of the church is prominent in Paul's epistle to the Ephesians. Our Lord Himself spoke of it, of course, when He said that He would build His church (Matthew 16:18). Paul defines and describes the church. For example, he says that God "put all things in subjection under [Christ's] feet, and gave Him as head over all things to the church, which is His body" (Ephesians 1:22–23). Paul likens the church to a building—not an ordinary building, but "a holy temple in the lord, . . . a dwelling of God in the Spirit" (Ephesians 2:21–22). As we sometimes sing,

> Elect from every nation,
> Yet one o'er all the earth,
> Her charter of salvation,
> One Lord, one faith, one birth;
> One holy name she blesses,
> Partakes one holy food,
> And to one hope she presses,
> With every grace endued.
> —Samuel J. Stone, "The Church's
>   One Foundation"

The church is not yet complete, but the building is going up. Every time a sinner is converted, a living stone is added to the walls. Someday it will be completed; and then, as the hymn says, "The great Church victorious/ Shall be the Church at rest."

The Nicene Creed, which dates to the fourth century, states: "We believe in one holy catholic and apostolic church." Thus, the Nicene Creed adds the words *one* and *apostolic,* listing four identifying marks of the one church of which all Christians are members.

The word *one* refers to the unity of the true church. In the days of Paul and the other apostles there was no organizational unity. The only unity to which the New Testament refers is spiritual unity. As Paul says, "We, who are many, are one body in Christ, and individually members one of another" (Romans 12:5). All true believers, no matter what their denominational affiliations, are members of the one church, the body of Christ. But no single organization or community of Christians is *the* church.

The word *holy* is an Anglo-Saxon equivalent of the Latin word *sanctified.* The root idea is "separation." In the Bible, even mountains could be designated as holy, meaning "set apart for God's purposes." Our Lord used the word of Himself in His prayer, when He said, "I sanctify Myself." He meant that He was consecrating Himself to the work He had come to do (John 17:19). "We believe in the . . . holy . . . church" means that we believe the church belongs to God.

It is also holy in the sense of being pure. No organized church ever has merited the designation *holy*—not in the past, and not now. Thus, the description belongs to the church as a whole, including its members already in heaven. Paul compares this church to a bride. Christ, the heavenly Bridegroom, "gave Himself up for her . . . that

He might present to Himself the church in all her glory, having no spot or wrinkle . . . but . . . holy and blameless" (Ephesians 5:25–27). No denomination fits that description.

Finally, the church is apostolic. If it were possible to trace a particular denomination's genealogy back to the apostles, that denomination could claim apostolicity. It is impossible to do that, but even if it were possible, a second test would be required: conformity to primitive teaching in its entirety. That is really the only test that is even remotely possible. Clearly, the word *apostolic* refers to Paul's description of the church as "having been built upon the foundation of the apostles and prophets" (Ephesians 2:20). In fact, the only truly apostolic church is the church that cannot be identified by a label or gathered together in one place. Its members live in every country, and millions have already gone home to heaven.

Even so, many denominations claim to be New Testament churches. They insist that their churches are modeled after the originals mentioned in Scripture and that they subscribe to apostolic teaching in its entirety. The members of such denominations believe that their practices most closely resemble those of the first-century apostolic churches. The truth is, the most that any group can *justly* claim for itself—including groups marked by stark simplicity—is that the group is *part* of the church that is Christ's body.

Accordingly, W. H. Griffith Thomas makes the point that "if . . . the question is asked: *Which* is the Body of Christ? it cannot be answered. But if enquiry is made, *Where* is the Body of Christ[?] it can be confidently said to exist wherever vital union with Christ is found."[2]

Thus, it is incorrect to think of any visible church or group of churches as "one holy catholic and apostolic church." That description, found in part in the Apostles' Creed and in the Nicene Creed, is true only of the *complete* church, which is necessarily neither local nor visible. In his epistle to the Ephesians, Paul speaks of the church as "one body" and "the whole body" (Ephesians 2:16; 4:16). It is visible only to God.

Nevertheless, the parts should exhibit some of the qualities of the whole. Every church should be characterized by genuine holiness, and every church should strive unceasingly to know and understand the New Testament in order to be as "apostolic" as possible.

Though no denomination is entitled to claim that it is truly apostolic, whereas other groups are not, believers in general will listen to that claim more attentively if the group in question manifests the graces and the fruit of the Holy Spirit of God (see Galatians 5:22–23). But if a single church or group of churches is marked by carnality, who is going to take its claims seriously?

The church is one, and it is holy; it is universal, and it is apostolic. It is God's church, which He purchased with the blood of His own Son. This is the church we have in mind when we say, "I believe in the holy catholic church."

The "one holy catholic and apostolic church" is the whole body of Christ, which cannot be gathered together in one place. Part of it is already in heaven, and the rest is scattered all over the globe. But any group of people who know and love Christ and give evidence of that in their lives and behavior may be safely designated a true church.

NOTES

1.W. H. Griffith Thomas, *The Catholic Faith* (London: Church Book Room, 1947), 55.
2.W. H. Griffith Thomas, *The Principles of Theology* (London: Canterbury, 1930), 277–78.

Chapter Twenty-Three

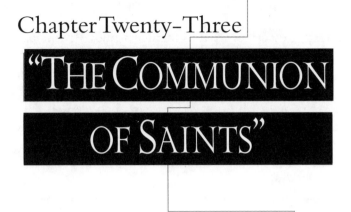

"THE COMMUNION OF SAINTS"

I believe in ...
The *communion of saints* ...

*W*hat do we mean when we say, "I believe ... in the communion of saints"? Before attempting to answer the question, two preliminary statements are in order: First, this clause of the Apostles' Creed is of later date than the rest.[1] Second, it has been interpreted in different ways. For example, Martin Luther took it to be a definition of "the holy catholic church." In his view, emphasis is laid on the word *saints,* whereby the *holy catholic church* is defined as a congregation of saints. A saint is one who belongs to God.[2]

However, if emphasis is laid on the word *communion,* Luther's interpretation is weakened. The Latin word *communion,* rendered *koinonia* in Greek, means participation in some common benefit. It does not define the church;

instead, it describes what its members enjoy—participation in certain blessings.

That, in my judgment, is the meaning of the clause. The preceding clause, "I believe in the . . . holy catholic church," states the unity that exists between all true believers. We are one in Christ. The clause now before us is not intended to say the same thing; instead, it gives the additional thought of communion, which means awareness of union.

We Christians are aware of our union with each other through union with Christ. If I am united in some way to Christ, and if you also are united to Christ, then we are united to each other. Because we are one, we have common interests and joys. Communion develops from awareness of union.

Christians who understand the meaning of union with Christ and with each other enjoy fellowship. They are aware of a common joy, a community of interests, and a mutual dependence upon each other. The saints—that is, you and I and every other true believer in Jesus Christ—do not live as individuals isolated from each other. We are not loners. We believe in and enjoy "the communion of saints."

Some of our hymns express this great truth. For example:

> For all the saints who from their labors rest,
> Who Thee by faith before the world confessed,
> Thy name, O Jesus, be forever blest.
> Alleluia! Alleluia!
>
> O blest communion, fellowship divine!
> We feebly struggle; they in glory shine.

Yet all are one in Thee, for all are Thine.
Alleluia! Alleluia!
—William Walsham How, "For All the Saints"

and

He wants not friends that hath Thy love,
And may converse and walk with Thee,
And with Thy saints here and above,
With whom forever I must be.

In the communion of saints
Is wisdom, safety and delight;
And, when my heart declines and faints,
It's raised by their heat and light.
—Richard Baxter, "He Wants Not Friends
   That Hath Thy Love"

That is what we mean, in part, when we say, "I believe in the communion of saints."

Certain confessions of faith elaborate on the concept. For example, the Westminster Confession says that every saint (i.e., every true believer) is "bound to maintain a holy fellowship and communion." The Westminster Confession sets forth the idea that every Christian is under obligation to seek the spiritual and temporal welfare of others.

That kind of communion is not to be restricted to members of one's own denomination. It should be extended, as opportunity is given, to all who call upon the name of the Lord. If that principle were practiced, it would greatly minimize the scandal of sectarianism. It may be impossible to avoid denominational affiliation, but all Christians should, with God's help, purge themselves of the sectarian spirit that rejects Christians not within the immediate group.

Most of us resist the charge of sectarianism. Nevertheless, elaborate church regulations make us sectarian in practice, if not in spirit. Take the concept of a closed Communion, which limits participation in the Lord's Supper to members of the denomination. Theoretically, the idea is to keep impostors out. In practice, it keeps Christians out.

Dr. Harry Ironside managed to rise above the sectarian spirit. When asked to identify his denomination, he said be belonged to the psalmist's denomination. What did he mean? Dr. Ironside quoted Psalm 119:63: "I am a companion of all them that fear thee, and of them that keep thy precepts" (KJV). That is the best denomination! Those who belong to that denomination can recite the Creed truthfully, "I believe in *the communion of saints.*"

NOTES

1. John Pearson, D.D. *An Exposition of the Creed* (London: Bell & Daldy, 1867), 533.
2. John Stump, *An Exposition of Luther's Catechism* (Philadelphia: United Lutheran), 107–9.

Chapter Twenty-Four

"THE FORGIVENESS OF SINS"

I believe in ...
The forgiveness of sins ...

$\mathcal{F}$orgiveness is one of the first blessings conferred upon a Christian, and accordingly, it has its place in the Apostles' Creed. We declare our belief in the forgiveness of sins. To forgive is "to give up claim to requital from [an offender]; to remit the penalty." Forgiveness and pardon are the same thing. Our English word pardon comes from a French compound word, meaning "to give up completely" (that is, thoroughly). In forgiving us, God gives up His sword, so to speak. He gives up His right to exact a penalty from us.

Everybody knows what sins are. The simplest dictionary definition of sin is "transgression of the law of God." In a secondary sense, sin is the violation of human laws. As used in the Creed, the word refers to the law of God and would include every form of sin against His laws. In the Creed, we affirm our belief in forgiveness of all our sins against God.

The concept is prominent in the Bible. Shortly after the Ascension of our Lord, the apostles announced that Jesus was ready to forgive Israel. Peter told the official council of the Jews in Jerusalem, "[Jesus] is the one whom God exalted to His right hand as a Prince and a Savior, to grant repentance to Israel, and forgiveness of sins" (Acts 5:31).

Paul's first recorded sermon was delivered in Pisidian Antioch. It was not a formal sermon; he was just talking with great earnestness to some of his compatriots in a synagogue. Near the end of his talk, he exclaimed that through Jesus forgiveness was being proclaimed (Acts 13:38). As Paul says elsewhere, "In [Christ] we have redemption through His blood, the forgiveness of our trespasses, according to the riches of His grace" (Ephesians 1:7). Thus, we believe in unlimited forgiveness, according to the riches of God's grace.

If Martin Luther or another of the Reformers of the church had written the Apostles' Creed, he might not have said, "I believe in the forgiveness of sins." Instead, he might have written, "I believe in justification from sins." Why? Didn't Luther and his friends believe in forgiveness?

The Reformers believed in forgiveness, as does every Christian who knows what the Bible teaches. Our hearts yearn for forgiveness, and the Bible tells us that God is forgiving. One of the loveliest passages in Scripture is Micah 7:18: "Who is a God like You, who pardons iniquity and passes over the rebellious act of the remnant of His possession? He does not retain His anger forever, because He delights in unchanging love." Our God pardons iniquity; He is forgiving.

However, we need more than forgiveness. We need acceptance; we need the assurance that we have a standing before God and that He will not turn against us because of our future sins. In short, we need all that justification implies. Justification is concerned with our standing before God. Seen from God's point of view, justification is a gift whereby God reverses the effects of sin and restores a relationship between Him and humankind that was lost in the Garden of Eden.

Theologians note three results of sin in Eden: guilt, condemnation, and separation from God. Justification is an act whereby God deals with those three things. First, He forgives us, in this way lifting the condemnation that hangs over us. Second, He removes our guilt by imputing righteousness to us. Finally, He ends our spiritual separation from Him by restoring us to fellowship with Himself.

Clearly, all that is much more than forgiveness. God not only forgives us, He also treats us as if we were righteous, and He brings us into His "family." That is what Paul had in mind in his series of questions in Romans 8. "Who will bring a charge against God's elect?" he asks (v. 33). Answer: No one! Guilt has been removed. "Who is the one who condemns?" (v. 34). Answer: No one! Condemnation has been lifted. "Who shall separate us from the love of Christ?" (v. 35). Answer: No one! Separation is ended, and reconciliation has been achieved.

All of that is included in justification, which is obviously broader than forgiveness. Dr. W. H. Griffith Thomas compares the two benefits in this way:

Justification is, therefore, much more than pardon, and the two are clearly distinguished by St. Paul (Acts 13:38–39). A criminal is pardoned, but is not regarded as righteous. But justification is that act of God whereby He accepts and accounts us righteous, though in ourselves unrighteous. The Christian is not merely a pardoned criminal, but a righteous man. Forgiveness is an act and a succession of acts; justification is an act issuing in an attitude. Forgiveness is repeated throughout the life. Justification is complete and never repeated. It relates to our spiritual position in the sight of God and covers the whole of our life, past, present, and future. Forgiveness is only negative, the removal of condemnation. Justification is also positive, the removal of guilt and the bestowal of a perfect standing before God. In a word, justification means reinstatement.[1]

It is easy to see why the Reformers and others might have changed the Creed, if it had been left to them to do so. But perhaps it is unnecessary to rewrite it. It is perfectly correct to say, "I believe in *the forgiveness of sins*," as long as we know that God has much more to give us than mere forgiveness.

NOTE

1. W. H. Griffith Thomas, *The Principles of Theology* (London, Canterbury, 1930), 185–87.

Chapter Twenty-Five

"THE RESURRECTION

OF THE BODY"

I believe in ...
The resurrection of the body ...

*E*very time we recite the Apostles' Creed, we affirm our belief in the resurrection of the body. We know that at death the human body begins to disintegrate and in time becomes dust, so that it is virtually inseparable from the elements in which it is buried. Nevertheless, according to our Christian belief, that same body will rise again.

Paul teaches that our bodies will be resurrected. In a lengthy chapter, 1 Corinthians 15, he speaks first of Christ's resurrection. Then he says that Christ's resurrection is the guarantee of every believer's physical resurrection. In Paul's thinking, Christ's resurrection and ours are so vitally linked that if one denies the possibility of our bodily resurrection, he must also deny that Christ rose from the dead (1 Corinthians 15:13, 16).

That is why the Creed includes a statement of belief in the resurrection of the body. Having said that "the third day He rose from the dead," the Creed must go on to affirm belief in our resurrection. You cannot have one truth without the other.

Christ's resurrection is also the model to which ours must conform. Paul explains that God, "who raised Christ Jesus from the dead will also give life to [our] mortal bodies through His Spirit who indwells [us]" (Romans 8:11). In another place he says that our resurrected bodies will be like Christ's resurrected body. The Lord Jesus Christ, Paul says, "will change these wretched bodies of ours so that they resemble his own glorious body" (Philippians 3:21 PHILLIPS 1972).

We believe that our bodies are important and that they have a future. Both of these ideas run counter to popular notions about the human body. The Greeks, whose views are still widely accepted, distinguished sharply between spirit and matter. Thus, in their judgment, fornication or adultery are sins of the body, and the spirit is unaffected by them. Eventually the body goes into the grave, from which it never emerges. The spirit lives on in the land of the dead.

The Bible also distinguishes between spirit and matter, but the connection between body and spirit is vital and permanent; human beings are not just spirits imprisoned in clay. Disembodied, we are "unclothed"—we are in some way incomplete—a defect, so to speak, that God will remedy at the resurrection of our bodies (2 Corinthians 5:1–4).

Meanwhile, the body is important. It is not only an intimate part of a human being, but it is also the instrument with which one may either glorify God or commit sin. The body can be "defiled," despite the truth that evil things proceed from within, from what the Bible terms "the heart" (Mark 7:14–23). The body, as well as the soul, can be cast into hell in judgment.

Paul was acutely conscious of the fact that the body contributes to the quality of life. He "beat" his body, to keep it from becoming a vehicle of sin and thereby destroying him. Paul was probably speaking metaphorically; he did not actually flog his body or wear a hair shirt. But he knew the power of bodily appetites, and he refused to allow them to dominate him (1 Corinthians 9:24–27).

He refused to defile his body. He asked believers in Corinth if they did not know that their bodies were "a temple of the Holy Spirit." Accordingly, Paul says, "You are not your own ... therefore glorify God in your body" (1 Corinthians 6:15–20). Our bodies are important to God.

The Bible speaks of the redemption and renewal of our bodies. Our bodies will be raised from the dead, and they will be changed. They will be immortal—never to die again—and they will be like Christ's resurrection body (1 Corinthians 15:53; Philippians 3:21).

After His resurrection, Jesus was no longer subject to the physical limitations generally associated with bodily existence. His body remained a body, but it was different. He could suddenly "materialize," as if He had walked through the walls. He could also vanish instantly, as if He had changed into air (Luke 24:31, 36). Although He had a real body, He did not get tired or sleepy or hungry.

We Christians will have that kind of body. As Paul

says, speaking of the resurrection of the body, "as is the heavenly, so also are those who are heavenly. Just as we have borne the image of the earthy, we will also bear the image of the heavenly" (1 Corinthians 15:48–49). When our bodies have been resurrected from the grave, we shall be like Christ.

When that is accomplished—at Christ's coming—then, as John says, "We will be like Him, because we will see Him just as He is" (1 John 3:2). Sin and its effects will have been sloughed off—left forever in the grave. Body and soul together, we shall be like Christ.

Chapter Twenty-Six

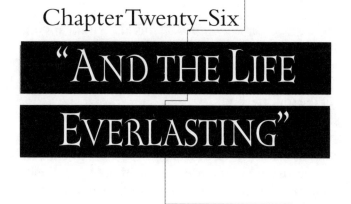

"AND THE LIFE
EVERLASTING"

I believe in ...
The resurrection of the body,
And the life everlasting ...

𝒯he connection between "the resurrection of the body" and "the life everlasting" is obvious. If our bodies are going to be raised, they will be raised for a purpose. The purpose is explained in Scripture in various places: that soul and body may be reunited permanently. Thus complete, we shall live forever.

Life is best understood in contrast to death. Death is separation. Spiritual death separates the soul from God. Isaiah says, "It is your sins that separate you from God" (Isaiah 59:2 TEV). Paul describes unregenerate people as "dead in [their] trespasses and sins" (Ephesians 2:1), distanced and alienated from God because of sin, which He detests (4:18; Colossians 1:21).

Physical death separates the soul from the body. Virtually every language expresses this idea. At the moment of death, friends keeping watch beside the bed say, "He's gone." Later, we say, "He passed," or, "He passed away." The immaterial part of the person leaves the body. Without the soul, the body is dead.

The second death is eternal death—the separation of the body and soul from God forever. This truth is taught in perhaps the most dreadful passage in the Bible, which predicts that everyone whose name is not written in the Book of Life will be thrown into the lake of fire (Revelation 20:11–15).

Eternal life is the opposite of death. The root idea is union, as contrasted with separation. Instead of being alienated, Christians are reconciled to God. Instead of dying, Christians are "made alive." As Paul says, "God's mercy is so abundant, and his love for us is so great, that while we were spiritually dead in our disobedience he brought us to life with Christ" (Ephesians 2:4–5 TEV).

We Christians believe in "the life everlasting" because the Bible says that is what God has planned for His people. Psalm 16 records a lovely confession of belief: "You will make known to me the path of life; . . . in Your right hand there are pleasures forever" (v. 11). The prophet Daniel foretold a day when "many of those who sleep in the dust of the ground will awake, these to everlasting life, but the others to disgrace and everlasting contempt" (Daniel 12:2). Daniel anticipated everlasting life, as well as its opposite: "Disgrace and everlasting contempt."

The Creed does not mention "disgrace and everlasting contempt." The Creed is a positive statement of truths held by Christians and essential to their development as believers. Nevertheless, belief in "the life ever-lasting" does not preclude its opposite. Anyone who takes the Bible at face value must believe what it says about eternal judgment.

Two verses in John 3 make the point clearly. First, verse 16: "For God so loved the world, that He gave His only begotten Son, that whoever believes in Him should not perish, but have eternal life." Now verse 36: "He who believes in the Son has eternal life; but he who does not obey the Son shall not see life, but the wrath of God abides on him."

Both verses make it clear that the choice is ours for either eternal life or eternal wrath. God offers life, and He does everything consistent with His nature to per-suade us to choose life. But He lets us choose.

I made the choice many years ago. If it were neces-sary to choose again and again, I would make the same choice each time: eternal life. But having made the choice once, I am eternally secure. Now all I need to do is testify to that choice, as we do when we recite the Creed.

I believe in God the Father Almighty,
Maker of heaven and earth:
And in Jesus Christ, His only Son, our Lord,
Who was conceived by the Holy Ghost,
Born of the virgin Mary,
Suffered under Pontius Pilate,
Was crucified, dead, and buried:
He descended into hell;
The third day He rose from the dead;
He ascended into heaven,

And sitteth on the right hand of God the Father
   Almighty;
From thence He shall come to judge the quick and
   the dead.
I believe in the Holy Ghost:
The holy catholic church,
The communion of saints:
The forgiveness of sins:
The resurrection of the body,
And the life everlasting.

Amen.

The last word, *Amen,* is a Hebrew word that should
be translated "Certainly!" or "It is so!" Thus, the *Amen*
looks back over the entire Creed and says, "That's right!
That is the truth, and that is what I truly believe!"

Can you say "Amen" to the entire Creed?

REVIEW AND STUDY GUIDE

INTRODUCTION

*T*he purpose of the Foundations of the Faith series is to reacquaint the reader with some of the great doctrines and favorite Scripture passages relating to our Christian life. Indeed, these books attempt to link together our faith as we understand it and our life as we live it. Though our goal is to provide more in-depth teaching on a topic, we hope to accomplish this with a popular style and practical application. Books in the series include the Lord's Prayer, the Ten Commandments, Psalm 23, and 1 Corinthians 13.

In keeping with our goal of a popular-level treatment, this review and study guide is not meant to involve exhaustive digging, but to reinforce the important concepts in the "Points to Consider" and to help you explore some of their implications in the "Question and Response."

A book's impact is judged in the long term, and if you can retain at least one important point per chapter and answer and act upon some of the questions relevant to your life, you have made considerable progress. May God bless your walk with Him as you enter into these exercises.

JAMES S. BELL, JR.

Chapter One

POINTS TO CONSIDER

1. The Creed is for all believers throughout history, but it is also a personal statement of faith within the context of worship.

2. Without clearly defined personal beliefs, you are just as lost as any outsider, even though you may be a church member.

QUESTION AND RESPONSE

1. What happens to our religious practices when truth is unimportant or missing?

Chapter Two

1. The existence of God can be arrived at in an orderly, rational fashion because He has revealed Himself this way.

2. We also have our direct experience of God to help confirm His existence.

3. Though His existence is evident, we still need to thirst for Him in order to know Him.

QUESTION AND RESPONSE

1. Of the four proofs mentioned, which has been most convincing for you in terms of God's reality?

Chapter Three

1. In the story of the Prodigal Son, God's nature is compared to the seeking father, who was full of love and forgiveness.

2. Though He continually reached out to them, Israel rejected its role as sons of the Father.

3. We are sons of God through faith in Jesus Christ alone.

QUESTION AND RESPONSE

1. Why do you think the nation of Israel was unwilling to play its ordained role of obedient children?

Chapter Four

POINTS TO CONSIDER

1. To be children of a Father who is almighty means to have a relationship with a loving God capable of total power in our lives.

2. God's power is never arbitrary or vindictive, but is always controlled by His warm and loving heart.

3. Though the Father is sufficient in Himself, He places all He has at our service, so that we may experience His fullness.

QUESTION AND RESPONSE

1. With the understanding that God is almighty, put before Him your most insurmountable problem and expect Him to respond.

Chapter Five

POINTS TO CONSIDER

1. Jesus Christ is the center of attention in the Apostles' Creed because His work is central to our faith.

2. The Creed implies the divine and human natures of Christ working together in harmony as one.

3. Jesus Christ means both "Jehovah saves" and "The Anointed One," our chosen Messiah.

QUESTION AND RESPONSE

1. Is Jesus anointed for a mission in your life? How is He both your Savior and your King?

Chapter Six

POINTS TO CONSIDER

1. Jesus is God the Father's unique son, but because of what He did for us we are now sons of the Father as well.

2. If you do not have a relationship with the Son, you cannot know the Father.

3. The Father and the Son are distinct persons, yet they are in complete union.

QUESTION AND RESPONSE

1. Is it possible to relate to God as Father?

Chapter Seven

POINTS TO CONSIDER

1. As Lord of all, Christ has supreme authority over all creation, for everything was created through Him.

2. Christ will not have exercised His authority fully until all His enemies are completely vanquished.

3. Confessing Jesus Christ as Lord is necessary for salvation, even though every knee will eventually bow to Him.

QUESTION AND RESPONSE

1. What areas of your life are not under the full sovereignty of the Lord Jesus Christ?

Chapter Eight

POINTS TO CONSIDER

1. At the moment of conception Jesus was originally and completely sanctified by the Spirit, without any taint of sin.

2. Although His conception was supernatural, the rest of the birth process was similar to other humans.

3. Christ is only one Person, not two, although He has two natures.

QUESTION AND RESPONSE

1. Does the Virgin Birth inspire you with awe and wonder at God's creativity? What other aspects of His character are displayed in this event?

Chapter Nine

1. The death of Christ and what it accomplished was more important than what He accomplished with His life.

2. Pilate declared Jesus innocent and yet, through his own self-interest, contributed to His suffering.

3. Christ suffered in many ways personally—through Satan and through the evil people who handed Him over to death.

QUESTION AND RESPONSE

1. Ask Christ's forgiveness for any disloyalty on your own part. When have you betrayed Him in thought, word, or deed?

Chapter Ten

POINTS TO CONSIDER

1. For all but Christians, the cross is a symbol of defeat, or all that is vile and shameful.

2. There are shadows, or types, of the cross predicted in the Old Testament, confirming the unthinkable notion that the Messiah would meet this horrible end.

3. Only complete humility and obedience could allow Jesus to endure this brutally painful death.

QUESTION AND RESPONSE

1. Visualize your own sins being laid upon Jesus on the cross, and worship Him for the greatest act of love ever known.

Chapter Eleven

POINTS TO CONSIDER

1. Christ chose to die before the foundation of the world, and He did it voluntarily under controlled circumstances.

2. The death of Christ will remain a reality for all eternity as we behold the person of the Lamb who was slain.

3. The future itself and our eternal destinies as creatures will be decided by our response to His death.

QUESTION AND RESPONSE

1. How do you explain the fact that as a believer you have also died and yet now live?

Chapter Twelve

1. With the sovereignty of God, each individual responds according to free will but also according to his or her fallen nature.

2. Our actions, whether good or evil, cannot ultimately frustrate the purposes of God.

3. Satan's dominion ended at the Cross, and with this in mind, he furiously attacked Christ as He suffered.

QUESTION AND RESPONSE

1. What was the main weapon that was taken away from Satan at the Cross? How does this free us?

Chapter Thirteen

1. God will not in any way excuse sin, and He exacted full payment at the Cross.

2. Christ's death provides a legitimate meeting place for a holy God and a sinful people.

3. Like Christ, we should empty ourselves of our status and rights and lay down our lives for others.

QUESTION AND RESPONSE

1. Have you responded to the death of Christ in the three ways the author states—belief, assurance, and service? Give examples.

Chapter Fourteen

POINTS TO CONSIDER

1. Eyewitness accounts of the burial of Jesus prove that He actually died.

2. In the Christian tradition, a dead body is sacred and should be treated in a respectful way.

3. The Old Testament account of the scapegoat sent into the wilderness is a prefigurement of Christ's burial.

QUESTION AND RESPONSE

1. The next time you seek forgiveness from God, view your sins as John Bunyan did—rolling down a hill into an empty tomb.

Chapter Fifteen

1. Christ did not go to hell upon death but may have released the spirits still in bondage that only He could set free.

2. The focus of this passage is that Christ's Spirit did not stay in His body while in the tomb but continued to work out His redemptive purposes.

3. We ourselves will not have to pass through any "holding place" for the dead, but because of Christ, we will be immediately with our Lord.

QUESTION AND RESPONSE

1. How have you dealt with the fear of death? Do you realize Christ has totally conquered its power?

Chapter Sixteen

POINTS TO CONSIDER

1. All other teachings in the Christian faith hinge on the truth of the physical resurrection of Christ.

2. The silence of His enemies and the boldness of His disciples add credence to Christ's resurrection.

3. The evidence for the Resurrection is so overwhelming that you can only deny it by saying miracles don't happen.

QUESTION AND RESPONSE

1. We are called to live a resurrection life. How do you view yourself as living in the context of the Resurrection?

Chapter Seventeen

POINTS TO CONSIDER

1. The Ascension goes beyond the Resurrection to establish Jesus as our high priest in heaven.

2. To the apostles, the Ascension was a joyful as well as a sad experience, for He promised His Holy Spirit and told them He would return to them soon.

3. Because of the Ascension, Christ is now able to be with us in all places at all times through His Holy Spirit.

QUESTION AND RESPONSE

1. What were the purposes of Christ's forty days on earth after the Resurrection?

Chapter Eighteen

1. Christ's work on earth is finished, but His priestly duties in heaven constitute His unfinished work.

2. Christ is "in session" for us; that is, He seeks to obtain all we need to successfully complete God's will for us.

3. Our focus should always be on things above, where we have full assurance that Christ will hear us and act on our behalf.

QUESTION AND RESPONSE

1. Explain your understanding of how Jesus Christ functions as your High Priest.

Chapter Nineteen

1. Compared to other important themes in Scripture, Christ's return is of critical importance, mentioned approximately three hundred times.

2. We often forget that we should not expect death, nor seek spiritual experiences, but rather seek to be rescued by the Lord's return.

3. Rather than concentrating on dates related to the Lord's return, we should focus on holy living in order to be ready.

QUESTION AND RESPONSE

1. Spend today and tomorrow living as though Christ were coming back within twenty-four hours, and review how this changes your walk with Him.

Chapter Twenty

POINTS TO CONSIDER

1. Christ is not only a Savior but a Judge who will determine the outcome of all things.

2. Christ will dispense rewards based on the circumstances of our lives—the opportunities, responsibilities, and privileges we've received.

3. We cannot know how God will judge those who have never heard the gospel. We do know that He is loving and fair to everyone.

QUESTION AND RESPONSE

1. Do heavenly rewards motivate you to holy living and service to Christ with all you have been given?

Chapter Twenty-One

1. The Holy Spirit was in the background in the Old Testament and the life of Christ, but is now prominent in the age of the church.

2. Without the Holy Spirit, God would not be evident to us—his forgiveness, new life, and power would not be comprehended.

3. Christ will raise us from the dead through the power of the Holy Spirit.

QUESTION AND RESPONSE

1. Have you thanked God for the many blessings that come your way because of the ministry of the Holy Spirit?

Chapter Twenty-Two

1. The true church of Jesus Christ is universal—sharing the same life and core set of beliefs around the world.

2. Although some denominations claim to be modeled exactly on the apostolic church, the most any group can claim for itself is that it is part of the church that is Christ's body.

3. God promises that His church will one day be complete and His purposes and plans will not be thwarted.

QUESTION AND RESPONSE

1. Have you pursued a spirit of unity with Christians from other denominations and traditions? Reach out to these other brothers and sisters in Christ.

Chapter Twenty-Three

1. Once we fully realize our union in Christ, we can develop fuller communion or fellowship with the saints.

2. Certain rules, such as closed membership for the Lord's Supper, create needless divisions, keeping other Christians out of fellowship.

3. As members of Christ, we cannot afford to be independent; God made us to need each other and each other's gifts.

QUESTION AND RESPONSE

1. Are you involved with other believers in a small group or other form of close fellowship? Make an effort to reach out to others and share deeply your life in Christ.

Chapter Twenty-Four

POINTS TO CONSIDER

1. Forgiveness of our sins is not enough; we need justification—counted as righteousness.

2. The term forgiveness can mean to "give up," and God does relinquish the right to demand payment for our sins because of Christ.

3. Through the Cross, God's forgiveness is unlimited, no matter how great the sin or how bad the sinner.

QUESTION AND RESPONSE

1. How should you respond, by using the justification doctrine, when you feel condemned for your sins, even after you have sought forgiveness?

Chapter Twenty-Five

1. Spirit is important, but so is matter (or our flesh). They cannot be separated, and that is why bodily resurrection is so important.

2. Our bodies should be respected and disciplined, for they are temples of the Holy Spirit.

3. We will have the same type of glorified body as Christ has, completely free of any of the effects of sin or mortality.

QUESTION AND RESPONSE

1. Thank God for the fact that although your body is imperfect or ill today, you will have a perfect body in heaven. Name some characteristics of this body.

Chapter Twenty-Six

POINTS TO CONSIDER

1. We die only once, but as believers we do not have to face the second death, the separation of ourselves everlastingly from God.

2. We must respond to the grace leading to everlasting life with God, or we will experience everlasting punishment, contempt, and disgrace.

3. Since God lives forever, if we are in union with Him even now, it means that we will dwell with Him eternally.

QUESTION AND RESPONSE

1. The Apostles' Creed ends in "Amen," or "It is so." Are you able to say "amen" because you better understand and are willing to put into practice the tenets of the Creed?